MANORS AND MANORIAL DOCUMENTS AFTER 1500

a guide for local and family historians in England and Wales

Mark Forrest

with Helen Watt

Manors and Manorial Documents after 1500

Published by the British Association for Local History 2022
Ground Floor, 4 Victoria Square
St Albans AL1 3TF
01625 664524
admin@balh.org.uk

© British Association for Local History 2022
www.balh.org.uk
All rights reserved

Typeset in ITC New Baskerville by John Chandler

ISBN 978-0-948140-06-8

The front cover illustration is a detail from Pieter Brueghel the Younger, The Payment of Tithes

The back cover illustration is from The National Archives, Parliamentary survey of Chertsey manor, Surrey, 1650 (reference E317/Surrey/9)

Contents

Acknowledgements		4
Preface		5
1	Introduction	7
2	The Structure of the Manor	9
3	The Lord of the Manor	15
4	The Manor Court Administration	17
5	The Court Baron	19
6	Tenants and Tenancies	27
7	The Court Leet	39
8	Stewards and Officers of the Court	42
9	The Customs of the Manor	49
10	Land Management Records Produced Outside the Court	55
11	The Relationship between Manors and Boroughs	70
12	The Changing Functions of Manors and their Courts	73
13	Case Studies Appearing in Works using Manorial Documents	80
14	The Manorial Documents Register and Access to Manorial Documents	83
Select Bibliography		85
Glossary		89
Key Dates		90
Photograph Acknowledgements		92
Index		91

Acknowledgements

This volume was compiled during the pandemic lockdowns of 2021 and 2022; we are most grateful to all the archivists who searched their image collections and provided information for the Guide. Not all of the material sent to us could be included; but we were pleased to receive a good range of documents to consult and from which to select images.

We would like to thank Kate Tobias-Buick (Cheshire Record Office), Robert Baxter (Cumbria Archive and Local Studies Centre), Becky Sheldon (Derbyshire Record Office), Anna Manthorpe and Christopher Whittick (East Sussex Record Office), Laura Russell (Glamorgan Archives), David Rymill (Hampshire Archives), Kate Rose (Kresen Kernow), David Tilsley (Lancashire Archives), Beth Elliot (Lincolnshire Archives), Daniel Williams (Northamptonshire Record Office), Mark Priddy (Oxfordshire History Centre), Oliver Lewis (Powys Archives), Liz Street (Staffordshire Record Office), the enquiry team at Worcestershire Record Office and Lord Shaftesbury for supplying images, information and permissions to reproduce documents from their collections.

We would also like to thank Heather Falvey who read an early version of the Guide and offered most helpful improvements and additional examples, John Chandler who has read, arranged and typeset the text, Jenny Day for her help with the transcript of the Glyndyfrdwy court book and Liz Hart, Steven Hobbs and Angus Winchester for comments, suggestions and additional material.

Mark Bailey has saved us from several errors and helped us to unpick the many technical aspects of courts, customs and tenures; he has provided clarification regarding the relationships between manors and boroughs and ensured that we were able to draw upon the most recent research. Additionally, he has been kind enough to write a preface to the Guide.

Mark Forrest and Helen Watt

Preface

The publication of this guide to post-1500 manorial records, aimed specifically at the needs of the local and family historian, is timely and propitious in three ways. First, it appears during the centenary year of the Law of Property Act (1922), which abolished copyhold tenure and, in so doing, effectively rendered manorial courts obsolete. Yet the records of these courts contained proof of title to former copyhold land, and so in 1924 an amendment to the Act required that manorial records should not be lost or destroyed and firmly placed them under the jurisdiction of the Master of the Rolls. In 1926 the Master of the Rolls published rules defining manorial documents and ordered a register to be kept of the nature and whereabouts of all such documents, thus ensuring their preservation in the United Kingdom. As a result of these statutory provisions, hundreds of thousands of manorial documents dating from the thirteenth to the twentieth century have been preserved and catalogued as part of our national heritage.

It is one thing to preserve documents and another to raise awareness of what exists and their whereabouts. During the twentieth century the details contained within the register of manorial documents were gradually expanded under the supervision of the Public Record Office (until 1959) then the Historical Manuscripts Commission. In 1992 the National Archives launched a project to load onto a database all the existing information relating to Wales within this paper-based register, which proved so successful that in 1995 its remit was extended to northern England. Since then, information relating to other English counties has been updated and added to the database. This online Manorial Documents Register provides professionals and the public with wider and remote access to detailed information about what manorial documents exist, for what manors, and where they are deposited. Furthermore, the online register is much easier to maintain and update than its paper-based predecessor. In 2022 this immense project to computerise and to enhance the information about surviving manorial documents will finally be completed for the whole of England and Wales. This is the second reason why the publication of this pamphlet is timely and propitious.

The third reason is that it fills a sizeable gap in the guidance available to local historians. Academic and local historians have exploited pre-1500 manorial documents extensively to reveal many aspects of everyday life in medieval England and Wales, and inexperienced researchers can benefit from the availability of various introductory guides to their form and content. In contrast, post-1500 manorial records have been relatively neglected. For example, there has been a pervasive sense that these later sources are rather uninformative, a view propagated by Sidney and Beatrice Webb in their seminal work on the manor and borough (1908). Furthermore, no updated and revised guide to post-1500 manorial records has been published for over four decades. Yet recent academic research has shown that post-1500 manorial documents can contain a considerable amount of useful information relating to the operation of local communities, and this brand-new guide helpfully surveys this new research.

The authors are well qualified to undertake this task on behalf of the British Association for Local History. Helen Watt has published a guide to Welsh manors (2000) and compiled the entries for the Welsh section of the online Manorial Documents Register for those documents held at the National Library of Wales.

Mark Forrest is an archivist who updated the entries for three English counties. The result is an attractive, well-illustrated, well-pitched and informative guide to these remarkable records. It should become the first point of reference for local and family historians, and if it encourages them to make greater use of the Register and the documents themselves, then it will have served its worthy purpose.

Mark Bailey
Professor of Late Medieval History, University of East Anglia
Chair, Manorial Documents Advisory Panel
February 2022

1
Introduction

Manorial documents are some of the most common records in English and Welsh archives. They contain a wealth of information about how people lived, worked, organised their communities and resolved disputes for over 700 years. They have been utilised extensively and primarily by medieval historians, which explains why they are not readily associated with research into early modern and modern history, yet the majority of surviving manorial documents were produced after the Dissolution of the monasteries in the 1530s. As a consequence, the researcher who is equipped with an understanding of how the manors and their courts operated can access a largely unexplored set of sources for petty crime, land holding, roads and bridges, public health, field names and genealogy which touch upon the lives of ordinary people resident in towns and villages across the country. While parish registers, tax records, census returns and wills can provide a framework of dates and events to look at past lives in the post medieval period, manorial documents can often develop these histories into fuller and richer biographies of individuals and communities.

The business of the manor was recorded in court rolls and books which were the formal records of the court. Additionally, there is a wide range of other documents: rentals, surveys, maps, accounts, lists of residents, custumals, perambulations of boundaries and the notes compiled by the steward, which fill in some of the gaps left by the official record. No two manors will have the same surviving set of documents; some will have court rolls while others have rentals, some have accounts and others perambulations, surveys were preserved for some while for others there are maps, and for some there are no remaining documents at all. Each manor is unique and each has a history that can be partly revealed through these sources. This handbook enables local and family historians to interpret those manorial documents that are written in English by examining the administration of the manor through the documents themselves. Establishing whether or what manorial documents exist for a given place, and where to find them, is now greatly facilitated by utilising the Manorial Documents Register, an online search engine supported by The National Archives cataloguing all the know extant manorial records in public and private archives across England and Wales.

The formal records of the courts remained in Latin until 1733, with the exception of the Commonwealth 1650-1659. However, many of the supporting documents, including the stewards' papers, surveys, rentals, rent rolls, presentments, perambulations, accounts and custumals began to be written in English from the start of the sixteenth century. By around 1600, most of these informal documents were in English, Welsh was rarely used.[1] So it is during the Tudor century and the Commonwealth that many local historians will begin to explore manorial documents.

Medieval manors have received far more attention from historians than post-medieval manors. Several guides are available to the medieval manor and its records which provide a good starting point for researchers looking at more recent records, as they show how manors had evolved up to the sixteenth century and

---

[1] A list of known Welsh documents is provided in Watt, *Welsh manors and their records*, 183-6.

At the opening of the Court.

Oyez, Oyez, Oyez. All manner of persons that do owe suit or service to this Court Leet, with a customary Court, or that were summoned to appear here this day, draw near and give your attendance, and answer every man to his name at the first call, and save your amerciaments.

2. Wareham manor, Dorset, circa 1900.
All manor courts involved a certain amount of theatre and ceremony. Most began with a proclamation made by the bailiff or steward like this example of a late C.19th opening of Wareham manor court:
Oyez, Oyez, Oyez. All manner of persons that do owe suit or service to this Court Leet, with a customary Court, or that were summoned to appear here this day, draw near and give your attendance, and answer every man to his name at the first call, and save your amerciaments.

how the variety of manors at that time had come into being.[2] Modern researchers and family historians are often unfamiliar with manorial documents, because publication of post-medieval manorial records by private individuals or county records societies is relatively rare. There are, however, notable exceptions, such as the records of the Manchester Court Leet covering the development of a northern rural manor into a sprawling urban settlement over 300 years.[3] The Yorkshire Archaeological and Historical Society has published a selection of court rolls for Wakefield dating 1274-1813,[4] there are a few examples of rural court rolls such as those for Brinkworth and Charlton (Wiltshire) and Church Lawton (Cheshire),[5] and there are many more publications of manorial surveys sometimes accompanied by contemporary maps.[6] Other perceived obstacles to using post-medieval manorial documents are that they are difficult to use or the dull administrative products of an administration in long decline. However, in the nineteenth and early twentieth centuries, the manor court was part of everyday life: Jane Austen and Thomas Hardy referred to manor courts and manorial documents in the expectation that their readers would understand their context without detailed explanation. When Beatrice and Sidney Webb examined the manor court as part of their epic study of

---

2   Bailey, *The English Manor*. Harvey, *Manorial Records*. Stuart, *Manorial Records*.

3   Earwaker, *The Court leet records of the manor of Manchester*.

4   The Yorkshire Archaeological and Historical Society produced six volumes of the Wakefield court rolls in their main series between 1901 and 1945 before establishing a separate series in which a further 19 volumes have been published. The 25 volumes contain documents from within the period 1274-1813 with each volume covering up to 24 years of courts https://www.yas.org.uk/Publications/Wakefield-Court-Rolls-Series.

5   Lawton, *Church Lawton manor court rolls*. Crowley, *Court records of Brinkworth and Charlton*.

6   See for instance Kerridge, *Surveys of the manors of Philip, earl of Pembroke and Montgomery* and Palmer, *Three Tudor Surveys*. Hervey, *Ickworth Survey Boocke*.

English local government, they were surprised to find 'manor courts that existed in 1689, many of which continued right into the nineteenth century, to be active local authorities, managing the common fields and pastures, suppressing nuisances, providing the police and trying cases of debt and trespass in little communities over which they had jurisdiction'. As they extended their research from county to county, they gained the impression that, in the late seventeenth century within the thousands of manors that still held courts, the maintenance of these functions was the rule and not the exception.[7] The functions of the courts gradually diminished and the number of courts was a fraction of what it had been four hundred years previously, but even into the nineteenth century, some courts still played a public regulatory role and an active part in estate administration, as well as managing commons, meadows and the tenancies of customary land. There is plenty of life in the post-medieval manor.

2
The Structure of the Manor

Manors have been part of the English and Welsh landscape for more than a thousand years and continue to function in a small number of administrative and legal areas. During this time, they have changed and developed, divided and merged, but the one constant factor in defining a manor has been the right of the lord of the manor to hold a manor court. In other words, manors possessed a dependent tenantry and some jurisdictional authority that required a local tribunal to regulate their business, which distinguishes them from other forms of landholding. The vast majority of manors were already in place by c.1300 and hardly any new manors were established thereafter, although by this date there was no formal definition of a manor. By the sixteenth century the manor had become defined in law as the area of jurisdiction of the manor court, and it had become accepted that a manor must also have existed 'time out of mind'.[8]

The origins of manors lie in the time between the end of the Roman Empire and the Norman Conquest. There are no written records of their origins, but by the time of the Domesday Book in 1086 they were already the basic unit of seigniorial landholdings (i.e. holdings of feudal lords) and most were intended to be self-sustaining and comprised land of different qualities.[9] At the most basic level, most contained land to grow crops, pasture animals, provide winter feed and produce wood for fuel and construction. To these might be added other local assets such as mills, fish ponds, dovecotes, the rights to extract minerals or the proceeds of wrecks washed up on a beach. Some manors consisted of discrete areas of land with a boundary that could be walked around in a perambulation. Others were composed of scattered plots with woods, meadows and common grazing often several miles from an arable centre and inter-mixed with different manors. They might contain an urban settlement (a town) and an urban institution (a borough) and some contained the whole urban area, such as Stanton (Hertfordshire), while a town such as Boston (Lincolnshire) developed over the land of four separate manors.

---

7   Webb and Webb, *English local government*, 116.

8   Harvey, *Manorial Records*, 2 and 55.

9   Bailey, *The English manor*, 5-18.

In 1279 a major survey of England, known as the Hundred rolls, show considerable variation in the size of manors for the counties where the rolls have survived: in Huntingdonshire 28 large manors, each with over 1000 acres of arable, accounted for 52% of the total arable area, 27 medium sized manors with 500-1000 acres of arable accounted for 22% of the total, and 134 small manors each containing less than 500 acres of arable made up the remaining 26%.[10] The figures for Buckinghamshire, Oxfordshire and Warwickshire are similar, although less pronounced, while in Cambridgeshire small, medium and large manors contained roughly equal acreages of the total available arable land. Despite occasional outliers it is possible to distinguish some regional variations. For example, this tract of central England was 'highly manorialised', in the sense that in 1279 every Cambridgeshire village contained more than one manor. Likewise in the west Midlands, because of the growth of population at Hanbury (Warwickshire) between 1086 and 1300 at least seven new manors were formed, as reserves of woodland were reclaimed and new manorial and landholding units created.[11]

In contrast, northern England and Wales were lightly manorialised, because it was much more common for large manors to encompass several settlements and because population growth before 1300 had not resulted in the creation of new manors. Wakefield manor (Yorkshire) covered over 150 square miles and was divided into twelve 'graveships' including Wakefield, Stanley, Alverthorpe, Thornes, Sandal, Osset, Horbury, Sowerby, Holme, Hipperholme, Rastrick and Scammonden.[12] In southern England, the Midlands and East Anglia, each settlement might contain several manors, whereas in the North and in Wales it was common for a single large manor to encompass several settlements.[13] This was not a clear-cut division: there were some very large manors in the south, particularly on royal estates or those of early monastic foundations, and some small manors in the north.

Manors came in many different sizes and their structure and composition were also highly varied. As we have seen, they might or might not include assets such as mills, warrens, turbaries, ovens, and dovecotes. At the core of the manor, was arable land and pasture, which belonged to one of three basic categories: the demesne, freehold and unfree land. The demesne was the lord's home farm, which the lord could opt either to exploit directly, using local people to help work the land and then consuming or selling the produce as he saw fit, or to lease some or all of land to any willing local lessee. Freehold land and unfree land (variously known by a number of terms such as customary, native, villein, or bond land) was held from the lord by dependent tenants in return for a defined rent package, which might include a cash rent, labour services on the demesne and other 'feudal' incidents such as marriage fines (merchets) or death duties (heriots). Tenants began to commute these services before 1086 for a money payment known as a quit rent, but there were also local terms such as 'worcsilver'; by 1300-49, only around 12% of manorial income was derived from work services and this declined over the following two centuries.[14] On manors where most services were commuted a few might be retained for the harvest: a series of custumals produced for the manors

---

10 Kosminsky, *Studies in the agrarian history of England*, 97-113.

11 Dyer, *Hanbury*, 27-43.

12 Fraser and Emsley, *Court rolls of the manor of Wakefield*, 1639-40, ix-xxviii.Fraser and Emsley, *Court rolls of the manor of Wakefield*, 1639-40, ix-xxviii.

13 Bailey, *The English manor*, 5-18.

14 Campbell, 'The agrarian problem in the early fourteenth century', 26-7.

of Shaftesbury Abbey includes harvest services being retained when week services were commuted for monetary payments between 1130 and 1170.[15] While free and unfree tenants owed both rent and some form of allegiance to their manorial lord, their land was protected from arbitrary seizure through various rights and customs. Exchanges of free land are not usually recorded in manorial courts, but instead were recorded in the royal courts and protected by the issue of a charter, whereas any exchange of customary land, or any issues relating to its use or dispute over its tenancy, had to be managed through the lord's court and nowhere else.[16] It was not until c.1600 that unfree land could be pleaded in the royal courts of common law.

Not all manors contained all three categories of land, or indeed a similar distribution of each category, which is one of the fundamental ways in which the structure of manors differed between and within regions. The 1279 Hundred rolls for Huntingdonshire, Cambridgeshire, Bedfordshire, Buckinghamshire, Oxfordshire and Warwickshire provide a useful indication of how medieval manors were structured at their peak: 32% of land was held in demesne, 40% by customary land and 28% in freeholdings, with significant differences between counties, 47% of land was customary in Huntingdonshire and only 29% in Cambridgeshire.[17] Those parishes consisting of a single manor, sharing the same borders, and particularly those on ecclesiastical estates, were more likely to have a larger numbers of customary tenants,[18] who might occasionally occupy all the land within a manor: in 1279 John Ewe's manor at Garsington (Oxfordshire) consisted of ten villein virgates each paying 13s 6d per annum and no demesne or freehold.[19] Overall, the larger manors tended to have a higher percentage of customary land and the small manors a higher percentage of demesne, but there is always an exception, such as the large Cistercian manor of Stoneleigh, Warwickshire which had 1,796 acres of arable freehold and only 14 acres of customary land. The small manor of Stoneleigh also contradicts the usual pattern of ecclesiastical manors generally being larger than those owned by the gentry.

Medieval demesne management shifted from direct administration by the lord and his officers to leasing, with the high point of directly managed demesnes around the start of the fourteenth century, then a gradual trend towards leasing, accelerated by the changes in the economy brought about by demographic decline.[20] When the demesne was no longer cultivated directly it might be broken up with some parts being converted to leasehold and others to copyhold. Whether it was directly managed or leased the demesne was generally the most profitable sector for the lord,[21] and it is usually presented as a separate area in surveys and extents of the manor even once it had been leased or broken up.

The development of Crown and estate administrations in Wales is an

---

15 Stacy, *The charters and custumals of Shaftesbury Abbey*, 29.

16 Bailey, *The English manor*, 28-9.

17 Kosminsky, *Studies in the agrarian history of England*', 89-95. Kosminsky highlights methodological problems with calculating the size of medieval holdings and the probable under representation of the demesne. Kanzaka's detailed re-analysis of the rolls suggests that nationally at least 46% and perhaps as much as 59% of land may have been freehold, Kanzaka, 'Villein rents in thirteenth century England', 599 and 611.

18 Kanzaka, 'Manorialisation and demographic pressure in medieval England', 11-23.

19 Kosminsky, *Studies in the agrarian history of England*', 84.

20 Campbell, *English seigniorial agriculture*, esp. 59-60, and 430-2.

21 Campbell, 'The agrarian problem in the early fourteenth century', 43-4.

extremely complex area and a comprehensive overview is provided by Rogers in his 'Introduction to the manorial system in Wales'. Manors developed in Wales rather later than in England, they were an English creation and imposition, common in the south and east before 1280 and later replacing the traditional Welsh divisions in the north.[22] They were introduced to all parts of Wales, but not everywhere was within a manor, and the Manorial Documents Register includes entries for the lordships and bailiwicks and their sub-divisions, that sometimes developed into manors, named raglotry, ringildry, bedellry or provostry after their officials. In Yale the ringildry (Yale Raglaria) and provostry (Yale Praepositura) were named after their respective officers, while at Wrexham four ringildries and a provostry, which partly reflected pre-Conquest kinship groups within Bromfeild and Yale lordship, are all represented on the Manorial Documents Register as manors.[23] In some cases these regions were divided between regions with English and Welsh inhabitants, Gower Wallicana and Gower Anglicana (Glamorgan); boroughs and their hinterlands were often administered separately and reflect not only the different forms of settlement, but also their division into primarily Welsh (rural) and English (urban) communities.

3. Detail from a map of Severn Stoke manor, Worcestershire, circa 1765.
The central section of this map shows the manor house, Clifton Court, with barn, outbuildings, fish ponds and orchards. Areas highlighted in green are the back gardens, closes and paddocks of the tenants. The open fields, divided into strips extend outwards from the village in red and blue.
An accompanying survey provides the names of the holders of each numbered plot.

---

22 Rogers, 'Introduction to the manorial system in Wales' 14-16.

23 Rogers, 'Introduction to the manorial system in Wales', 17.

Across much of England and in parts of Wales the manor had several large open fields, in which the tenants had blocks of arable, or common fields in which strips belonging to the tenants and the demesne were intermixed.[24] Open and common fields were most frequent in a band running down the centre of the country from the north-east to Somerset and Dorset, and in south Wales; although examples of these and other distinct regional field types, sometimes involving folding for animals, may also be found in East Anglia, Kent, Yorkshire and other northern counties.[25] There might be two, three, four, of more fields within a system which might change over time to add or enclose fields: Great Corringham (Lincolnshire) had two fields c.1200, which had been changed to a four field system before 1601 when they were re-arranged into a three field system.[26] Manors in the central band continued to play an important role in the day to day management of common field systems until the latter's disappearance through Parliamentary enclosure. Open fields could still be found in many parts of the country when the tithe maps were produced in the early nineteenth century and the last remnants of these field types can still be seen at Braunton Great Field (Devon) and Laxton open field system (Nottinghamshire).

Manors with open field systems and those without both had some land or resources that were regulated through the manor including meadows, woods, wastes and various forms of common grazing. Some of this land was 'several', i.e. its exploitation and access was restricted solely to the person who held the land. Most, however, was 'common', meaning that the lord, freeholders and customary tenants possessed rights to access and use the land according to various local arrangements. For example, manorial tenants might have the common right to access woodland, take nuts, graze animals, and collect fallen branches for fuel at certain times of the year, while the timber itself was strictly the reserve of the lord. Similarly, common rights to graze animals on pastures were prized and hence carefully regulated. The amount of arable possessed by each tenant might determine the number of animals that could be put onto the common, meadow might be divided by drawing lots or by rotation. At Congresbury and Puxton (Somerset), two large pieces of common land called East and West Dolemoors were divided into acres, each bearing a particular cut on the turf such as a horn, pole axe, duck's next, hare's tail, or four oxen and a mare.[27] A number of apples were prepared and, having been marked with the same symbols, were distributed to the tenants by a small boy from a hat or bag. After the distribution the tenants took possession of their allotment and gathered at the house of the 'overseer of Dolemoors', an officer elected annually by the tenants, where a further four acres, reserved for expenses, were leased by auction and the remainder of the day was spent in 'sociability and hearty mirth'.

Many manors had a manor house: either the residence of the lord or a designated court house. In some manors, there are several manor houses where one out-dated building was superseded by a more modern or fashionable dwelling. Occasionally the construction of the new manor house or the site of the old manor may be mentioned in the manorial documents or visible on contemporary maps. Most manors were owned by a non-resident lord who had no need of a manor house. The Webbs found that courts might be held beneath an ancient tree, in a barn of

---

24 Oothuizen, 'The Anglo-Saxon kingdom of Mercia and the origins and distribution of common fields' 154-6.

25 Hall, *The open fields of England*, 1-86.

26 Hall, *The open fields of England*, 41

27 Collinson, *History of Somerset*, v.3, 586.

4. Holdenby manor, Northamptonshire, 1580.
The new manor house and the site of the old manor house shown as dotted lines where the walls had stood (top left).

the manor farm, in the manor house, in a building known as the court house, a town hall or a guild hall.[28] It was common practice to open the court session at the traditional location and immediately relocate to the largest room in the village inn, particularly when the original site was outdoors.

Besides the physical components there were also certain rights that might be attached to a manor. The right to minerals below the sub-soil was almost universal to all manorial lords, in most areas this meant that the lord controlled the local stone and lime quarries, but sometimes there might be a more valuable resource such as the marble extracted on the Isle of Purbeck. The right to hold a weekly market or seasonal fair could be granted by the Crown to the lord of a manor who then charged tolls, rented stalls and issued fines for market offences through his court. Other rights depended upon local conditions, such as the coastal manors which had rights to the wrecks and whales washed up on the shore. course, The most important right was to hold a manor court. Every lord of a manor had the right to hold a Court Baron, attended by all of the unfree tenants of the manor and sometimes the free tenants too, to protect the lord's rights, to resolve certain types of disputes, to regulate the management of some communal resources, and to manage the communal and customary rights of the manor and the tenants. On some manors the Court Baron was held as frequently as every three weeks at its medieval peak, but after 1500 it was usually held once or twice a year. In addition, one manor within a given place also held the right from the Crown to hold a Court Leet, which was the lowest court of royal jurisdiction franchised to one local manorial lord. Leets were often run alongside manorial courts and by the same lord, and indeed were sometimes merged into one session, but in strict terms the two jurisdictions were separate, the attendance was different, and the business was also distinct (see Sections 4 and 6, below).

---

28   Webb and Webb, *English Local Government*, 17-18, 65.

3
The Lord of the Manor

Each manor had a lord, or lady, who had rights to hold the manor from a superior lord (and thence up a feudal ladder to the King), to pass the manor onto heirs or to sell it to a third party. The lord of the manor was, however, required to fulfil the terms on which it was held from their superior lord, otherwise the default could lead to its forfeiture or seizure. There were also other rights to observe, such as the right of the Crown to hold a manor temporarily during the vacancy of a bishopric, for example, or as ward to an underage heir. Lords of manors might be individuals of varying rank such as a leading earl of the realm, or a humble member of a gentry family, while others were perpetual institutions, such as an abbey or school.

The Crown possessed a large estate made up of dozens of manors throughout England and Wales known as the Royal or Ancient Demesne. Other manors defaulted to the Crown through wardship or confiscation and were managed on its behalf by the Court of Augmentations for short periods until the land was granted to an heir or redistributed to another aristocratic family. The Duchy of Cornwall was traditionally granted to an immediate member of the King's family, and included manors not only in Cornwall, but also in Devon, Dorset, Herefordshire, Hertfordshire, Norfolk, Oxfordshire, Surrey, Warwickshire, Wiltshire and Yorkshire. Other institutional lords such as the Church, schools and universities were endowed with manors at their creation or by later benefactors. Eton College held the manors of Great Blakenham (Buckinghamshire), Modbury Priory and Penquit (Devon), Charlton Parva, Piddlehinton and Povington (Dorset), East Wretham in Norfolk, Everdon (Northamptonshire), Adderbury and Little Tew (Oxfordshire), Yenston in Somerset, Chattisham and Creeting St Mary (Suffolk), Coldra alias Bulmore and Goldcliff (Monmouthshire). Most of these manors were former possessions of dissolved alien priories and had been granted to the newly founded Eton college by Henry VI. Despite substantial changes to the structure of many estates, the Church continued to be a manorial lord beyond the Reformation. The Archbishopric of York surrendered 14 manors in Northumberland and eight in Gloucestershire to the Crown in 1545, exchanging them for former monastic manors mostly in Yorkshire, which were added to the 30 manors it already held in the county.[29] The consolidation of the Archbishop's estate would have been greater but several manors were restored to the See in Mary's reign; including seven Nottinghamshire manors that had been given up as part of the same exchange.

The Dissolution of the monasteries had the twin effect of removing some of the most conservative manorial lords and introducing large areas of land to the market. Whole manors were granted to long-established families while others were purchased by an emerging group of merchants who speculated in property and used it as security for their transactions, and by the farmers who had previously held the demesnes by leases. The courtier Thomas Kitson was not unusual in acquiring several monastic manors and using stone from a dissolved priory at Ixworth to construct his substantial new manor house at Hengrave, Suffolk.[30] Other monastic manors were used as endowments for existing and newly-founded schools and colleges some distance from the institution itself. Eton and Winchester schools,

---

29 Cross, 'The economic problems of the See of York', 64-83.

30 Gage, *The history and antiquities of Suffolk*, 214.

Gonville and Caius College, Cambridge, and the Queen's College, Oxford, all received manors in south Dorset.

Records of manors held by institutional lords often survive in greater numbers than those of the gentry, because they were perpetual institutions with administrative continuity and space to accommodate large collections of archives. Gentry lords certainly maintained manorial records, but changes of ownership, limited resources and a smaller bureaucracy meant that their records have not survived to the same extent. The 'gentry' was a term covering a range of lords and ladies of different status, from minor local figures with perhaps just a couple of manors to wealthy individuals comparable to higher status people with many manors scattered over several counties. The archive of the Kitson, and later Gage, families of Hengrave Hall in Suffolk contains records for eighteen Suffolk manors, as well as one in Cambridgeshire, four in Devon, three in Dorset, six in Somerset and one in Yorkshire. When surveying ownership of manors in 1561 in the seven counties of Bedfordshire, Buckinghamshire, Hampshire, Hertfordshire, Surrey, Worcestershire and the North Riding of Yorkshire, R. H. Tawney found that 242 were held by the Crown, 335 by peers of the realm, 1,709 by the gentry, 185 by ecclesiastical institutions, 67 by schools and hospitals and nine by other individuals or organisations.[31]

The identity of each manor administered as part of an estate was almost always maintained when they were geographically separate and they often remained distinct when their lands were adjacent or intermixed. However, some manors which shared common fields or were located within the same parish might be merged into a single, larger, manor when they were held by the same lord. This process began as early as the eleventh century, but later mergers are easier to identify. Often it occurred when one lord acquired two neighbouring manors that had previously been held by two different lords and their merger enabled him to hold one series of courts and to appoint one set of officers. Small gentry held manors were also more likely to amalgamate than the larger institutional manors; the two adjacent manors of Durweston and Knighton (Dorset) became the single manor Durweston cum Knighton (the Latin *cum* meaning 'with') in the fifteenth century. Once combined, they held a single court, but with no realignment of the two sets of common fields, closes and tenements, or of the precincts into which they were divided.[32] At Lytchett Minster (Dorset), the parish originally contained four manors consisting of inter-mixed closes, by the fifteenth century two, held by the Kitson family, had been unified as Lytchett cum Beere and two others, were held by the Trenchards, as Slepe cum Cockamore.[33] Sometimes several adjacent or intermixed manors might be merged: within the parish of Hunstanton (Norfolk) the Lestrange family acquired three of the four manors by the end of the fifteenth century and brought them together as a single unit.[34]

English law relating to the inheritance of freehold estates meant that a manor always passed to the eldest son on the death of their father, although a widow may hold it during her lifetime. Despite this, if a lord had no sons it passed to his daughters and if there were more than one daughter it was divided equally between them. Because the manor could not be physically divided, each of three daughters would possess the lordship of a third of every field, a third of every house, of every mill and every other asset. The ownership and lordship of a manor

---

31   Tawney, 'The rise of the gentry: a postscript', 91-7.

32   Palmer, *Three Tudor Surveys*, 60-1 and 144-80.

33   Palmer, *Three Tudor Surveys*, 14.

34   Bailey, *The English manor*, 10.

might remain divided for several generations, or one of the co-heiresses might buy out the others an example of this complicated arrangement may be found at St Catherine's manor in Ruislip (Middlesex). St Catherine's manor was purchased by John Child, a London banker in 1719, it passed to his son Christopher and then to his four nieces. One of these, Sarah Mico, married John Lewin, who bought out the other three holders in 1768 and became the sole lord of the manor. In 1800, the lordship of the manor was again divided, this time into two parts, between Sarah and John Mico's daughter Sarah Lewin and their son-in-law William Sheppard, husband of their daughter Susanna, and the lordship remained divided between these two families until it was broken up in the later nineteenth century.[35]

Most manors held by church bodies were standard manors, structured as described above, but some were 'rectory' or 'parsonage' manors. These comprised the glebe lands of the parish church and other agrarian resources, and also included some sub-tenants of the glebe or of other parcels of land donated to the parish church, whose purpose was to provide the stipend of the priest and funds for the maintenance of the chancel. These were usually much smaller than other manors, and possessed a narrower range of non-arable assets, but they could be surprisingly numerous. In Norfolk at least 23 of the 451 manors where there was still copyhold land in 1835 were rectory manors.

4
The Manor Court Administration

Two different courts could be held regularly on the manor: the Court Baron and the Court Leet, supplemented by courts held regularly for a single purpose and special or extraordinary courts as required. All manors had a Court Baron and it is this court which defined the manor. Some manors also had the right to hold a Court Leet, a right originally devolved onto the lord of the manor from the Crown. The formal records of the courts, manor court rolls, survive in great numbers; the earliest date from the mid-thirteenth century and on some manors, they were produced regularly into the twentieth century. Although the records of the manor court are described as 'court rolls', from the later sixteenth century, the business of the courts was usually copied into books. When a manor remained in the hands of a single family or institution, a long series of rolls might survive covering several centuries. For instance, the manor of Kibworth Harcourt (Leicestershire) was held by Merton College, Oxford, where the court rolls from 1276 to 1888 are still kept in the college's archive in an almost complete sequence. While the Kibworth Harcourt series is unusual, it is not unprecedented, every county contains manors for which records survive in sequences spanning several hundred years and in most counties there is a good range of documents from the thirteenth through to the nineteenth centuries.

The records of the Court Baron and Court Leet were written up by the steward or his clerk as fair copies compiled from draft notes made during the court. The medieval record of the court in session, the court rolls, were rolled parchment membranes and on some manors they continued in this format into the seventeenth century. Later records produced in books were still termed 'court rolls'. Prior to the court presentments were submitted by the jury, officers and

---

35   Bolton, King, Wyld and Yaxley, 'Ruislip: Manors and other estates', 135-6.

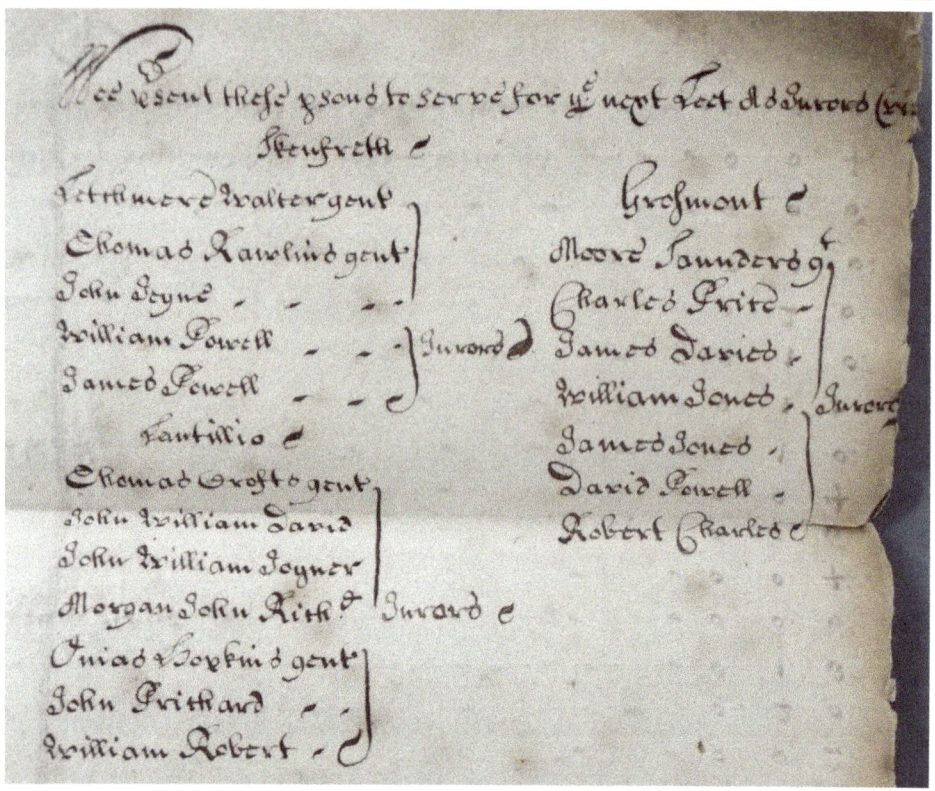

5. Jury summons, Three Castles Manor, Gwent, 1696.

Wee p[re]sent these p[er]sons to serve for the next Leet As Jurors (viz:)

Skenfreth		Grosmont	
Letchmere Walter gent		Moore Saunders g[en]t	
Thomas Rawlins gent		Charles Price	
John Jeyne		James Davies	
William Powell	Jurors	William Jones	Jurors
James Powell		James Jones	
		David Powell	
Lantillio		Robert Charles	
Thomas Crofts gent			
John William David			
John William Joyner			
Morgan John Richard	Jurors		
Onias Hopkins gent			
John Prichard			
William Robert			

customary tenants (known as the '*homage*'), these were then copied into the rolls along with any adjudications made in the court. Their contents vary considerably over time depending upon changes in business of the manor court, such as whether it regulated the commons before and after enclosure. The primers which had been used by stewards across the country since the thirteenth century introduced a high degree of standardisation to the court processes and this national standardisation was increased by the stewards of larger estates which owned manors in several different counties who travelled around circuits of manors.

As well as the records compiled during the court in session the steward kept files of notes, papers and extracts of court rolls relating to particular issues such as inheritance, the next heirs to properties and the ages of people named in tenancies held for lives. They also compiled and retained formal documents, produced outside the court, to assist in managing the manor including surveys, rentals, rent rolls, maps, extents, perambulations, custumals and accounts.

The court was always held within the manor, but on larger manors it was was sometimes divided into sections representing different areas. At Leven in the East Riding of Yorkshire there were two separate juries: one from the urban centre and another for it's rural hinterland. On the other hand, at the Three Castles manor (Gwent), a single jury was empanelled with representatives from each of the three divisions of the manor.

The names of courts varied between manors. The Court Baron might be known as the manor court, hallmoot, customary court, little court or tenants' court. Special sessions of the Court Baron were held for specific purposes: a court of estrays was held regularly on those manors with widely dispersed livestock, courts of survey were held so a surveyor could seek information from tenants and a court of recognition was sometimes held as the first court of a new lord. The Court Leet was sometimes called the great court, legal court or lawday. Market courts, also called pie powder courts, could be held as a separate session, attached to the Court Leet for frequent markets or fairs in larger towns or attached to the Court Baron when markets and fairs were held less often.

The technical and legal divisions between the courts were not always maintained and functions that might be normally associated with one type of court might be found in another. Officers of one court might also be appointed in another concurrently. The Webbs noted that by the start of the nineteenth century, and perhaps much earlier:

> courts calling themselves nothing but Court Baron [were] nevertheless appointing headboroughs, constables, ale-tasters and scavenger; making presentments on all sorts of subjects; and seizing light weights and short measures. We find courts calling themselves nothing but courts leet nevertheless appointing reeves and haywards and a variety of functionaries whose business it was to manage common pasture.[36]

Some courts that had clear and precise roles three or four centuries earlier had developed and combined into hybrid institutions, adopting functions from one another and held in a single session. Others maintained a clear distinction with the Court Baron dealing exclusively with estate management and the Court Leet with local government and law enforcement

5
The Court Baron

The Court Baron was the lord's court for all matters relating to the management of his manor. Although this had been held as frequently as three-weekly at the manor's peak in the fourteenth century, by the sixteenth century most were held perhaps four times a year, and in the seventeenth and eighteenth centuries, many courts were only held once or twice each year, usually to coincide with Michaelmas

---

36 Webb and Webb, *English Local Government*, 70.

(29 September) and Lady Day (25 March), when rents were due and the Court Leet was also held. In the eighteenth and nineteenth centuries, some courts were summoned only when changes in the tenants holding copyholds needed to be recorded, which might mean that the court was not in session for several years.

The court roll recording the Court Baron was usually drawn up according to a recognised formula which might vary from one manor to another, but always included the same elements. First, the heading provided core information about the court, often including the name of the manor, of the lord, of the steward and the date on which the court had been held. This was followed by apologies for absence (*essoins*); a list of the homage and / or jury; the names of those people who were obliged to attend court (*suitors*) and who were not present, together with their fines for non-attendance (*amercements*). Then followed the presentments of matters heard by the court, usually grouped into categories: property transfers, debt cases, incidents of trespass and recording stray animals. These might be followed by a recital of customs relating to topical concerns, appointments of officers and regulatory proclamations such as the dates when animals could be moved into different pastures. Finally the names of the two jurors who assessed the levels of fines (*affeerers*) were named, followed by the sum of money collected at the court.

The authority of the court regarding customary rights, obligations and restrictions was binding upon all tenants and its judgements required mutual agreement and acceptance between tenants and landlord. This led to the direct involvement of the customary tenants in making and enforcing the regulations, often through the oral testimony of the older tenants. Each manor court had a presentment jury chosen from the homage usually, but not always, of twelve men who were listed in the court roll. From their number two affeerers were selected who determined the penalties imposed for misdemeanours. The Court Baron might adjudicate on matters as diverse as the division of wrecks on the beach, enforcing fishing rights in rivers, movement of livestock, where brushwood was to be collected for fuel, allowing timber to repair buildings, defining paths, maintaining fences and hedges, selecting officers of the court and ensuring that trees were not felled without permission. These were all areas in which agreement and consent between neighbours was far preferable to legal enforcement and the fines imposed by the affeerers were often conditional if an action was not performed by a specified future date. The consent of the community was partly based upon the knowledge that the jury, affeerers and officers were all drawn from the homage, sometimes serving in rotation, so all tenants could at some stage be presented for an offence, be called upon to make a judgement, set a fine or enforce a decision of the court. On smaller manors all participants were almost certainly related, neighbours or otherwise well known to each other.

6. Harrington manor, Cumbria, 1734.
Ann Key being presented at the Prosecution of Thomas Bacon for Stopping her Watercourse whereby the s[ai]^d Thomas is greatly dampnified [damaged]. *We find the s[ai]^d Presentment to be true, And do Order the s[ai]^d Ann Key to Cleanse & Drain her Watercourse before the first day of June next, on Penalty of Three Shillings and four pence.*

The Court Baron was the lord's own court through which the property of the manor was managed. The most important function of the Court Baron was to regulate and record transfers of land: issuing copyholds, resolving disputes relating to inheritance or transfer, and recording the collection of death duties (*heriots*) and fines paid by new tenants (*entry fines* for customary tenants, *reliefs* for freeholders). On some manors customary tenants were obliged to obtain a licence to sub-let their lands. Heirs to copyholds established their claims through the Court Baron and the terms and conditions by which they were held were recorded in the court rolls. Sometimes this might mean referring to court rolls of previous decades to establish an individual's claim to a tenement or making reference to the customs of the manor to decide whether a claimant met the appropriate customary qualifications. Many courts also maintained a record of when freeholds and leaseholds changed hands, particularly when a payment was due to the manor, although these transactions took place outside the court.

Presentments recording those items brought to the court by the homage and the manorial officers were sometimes drawn up before the court took place and then copied into the court rolls. On some manors, where most of the formal records of the court in session were in written up in Latin, the presentments might be in English from the end of the sixteenth century, on others the presentments, written in English, survive in separate files. Presentments were recorded in the court rolls and kept separately as loose papers, bound into a discrete volume or filed by the steward with other useful items such as rent rolls, jury lists, oaths of officers and lists of tenants. The presentments of the officers, jury and homage are sometimes accompanied by proclamations, by-laws and orders issued by the steward.

Where the Court Baron and Court Leet were held together in the same session it is often difficult to distinguish those matters that fell within the remit of each court. In an examination of 6533 presentments, orders, by-laws and fines from 113 manors across England between 1550-1850, Waddell divided the offences he encountered into seven categories: violence and disorder, trade and crafts, immigration and accommodation, agricultural resources, non-agricultural resources, infrastructure and miscellaneous nuisances. Violence and disorder such as assaults, fights, gaming and scolding, sometimes directed against the court itself, were never common presentments. Those relating to craft and trade generally concerned regulations of millers and butchers, producers and sellers of beer, bread and leather; regulation of immigration and accommodation prevented sub-letting without licences, harbouring strangers and vagabonds, or erecting cottages on waste ground. More common were the presentments relating to agriculture which included regulating the common fields and common grazing and safeguarding those resources from external users or encroachments by tenants. Waddell separates the exploitation of natural resources such as timber, fish, building materials and various types of fuel from the agricultural presentments as these made up around 7% of all presentments. The largest group were those relating to infrastructure, including paths, ways, lanes, hedges, fences, dikes, ditches, folds, pounds, houses and roofs; finally there was a broad range of miscellaneous nuisances from causing risk of fire, or putting contagious animals into shared pasture to inappropriate waste disposal.

The presentments brought before the court might vary according to local circumstances. In Yorkshire, 1550-1850, the lowland manors required more intense supervision of common fields and 56% or presentments related to infrastructure, while on the upland manors only 26% of the presentments fell into this category;

A Presentment of the Homage of Sturminster Newton Castle at the Court Baron of the Right Honourable Lord Rivers Lord of this Manor held at the Kings Arms the 27th Day of October 1783.

They present that Peter Walter Esqr. heretofore made an Encroachment upon a small Piece of Land belonging to the Lord of this Manor and that the same is now continued by Lord Paget.

Also They present that no Person shall keep any Geese or Ganders in Puxey Common within this Manor under the Penalty of two Shillings and sixpence for every such Offence

Also They present that no Person shall stock with more Cattle in the Commons than they can winter on what they occupy in the parish of Sturminster Newton

Also They present that none of the common Meads shall be stocked but at the old usual Times without the Consent of all the Tenants.

Also They present the Commons to be fed with Sheep at the usual Times (from the 12th Day of November to the 6th Day of April following) and not otherwise under Penalty of Impoundment

Also They present Mr Thomas Read — to serve the Office of Hayward for Fryers Moore Mead for the Year ensuing
Daniel Rose sworn to execute

Also They present Jos. Newman — to serve the Office of Hayward for Tilbridge Mead for the Year ensuing

Also They present ~~Joseph Newman~~ Robert Rose to continue to serve the Office of Hayward for Southley Mead for the Year ensuing

Also They present Thomas Roberts Senr. to serve the Office of Hayward for Steart Mead for the Year ensuing

Also They present ~~Thomas Hunt~~ James Hchison to serve the Office of Hayward for Benditch Mead for the Year ensuing

Also They present Wm Colbourne to continue to serve the Office of Hayward for Sandmoore Mead for the Year ensuing

7. Sturminster Newton Castle manor, Dorset, 1783.

A typical set of late eighteenth century presentments demonstrates the largely agricultural concerns of the homage; unlicensed enclosure, common grazing and appointments of officers to manage the meadows.

A Presentment of the Homage of Sturminster Newton Castle at the Court Baron of the Right Honourable Lord Rivers, Lord of the Manor, held at the Kings Arms the 27th Day of October 1783.

They present that Peter Walter esqr. Heretofore made an encroachment upon a small piece of land belonging to the Lord of this Manor and that the same is now continued by Lord Paget.

Also, They present that no person shall keep any Geese or Ganders in Puxey Common within the Manor under penalty of two Shillings and sixpence for every such offence.

Also They present that no person shall stock with more Cattle in the Commons than they can winter on what they occupy in the Parish of Sturminster Newton.

Also They present that none of the common Meads shall be stocked but at the old usual times without the Consent of all the Tenants.

Also They present the Common to be fed with Sheep at the usual Times (from the 12th Day of November to the 6th Day of April following) and not otherwise, under penalty of Impoundment.

Also They present Mr Thomas Bird to serve the Office of Hayward for Fryers Moore Mead for the Year ensuing.

/Daniel Rose sworn to execuite[?]/

Also They present \Sir/ Jos[ep]h Newman to serve the Office of Hayward for Filbridge Mead for the Year ensuing.

Also They ~~Joseph Newman~~ \Robert Rose to continue/ to serve the Office of Hayward for Southley Mead for the Year ensuing.

Also They present ~~Thomas Chuitt~~[?] \Sir James Alchison/ to serve the Office of Hayward for Benditch Mead for the Year ensuing.

Also They present W[illia]m Colbourne to serve the Office of Hayward for Sandmoore Mead for the Year ensuing.

this pattern appears to be replicated in other counties.[37] There were also differences between urban and rural manors, with the former hearing far more presentments relating to trades and crafts, and to violence and disorder, whereas the latter were more concerned with agriculture and infrastructure; perhaps surprisingly close proximity made little difference to miscellaneous nuisances.[38] Agricultural presentments were not entirely absent from urban manors as most towns had a significant rural hinterland and rights to commons, pasture or arable.[39] Sometimes a series of presentments might cross over between the different roles of the Court Baron and Court Leet. An encroachment onto a neighbours property or a trespass with animals into a field of crops might lead to a violent dispute and charges of abuse and affray, and it is not uncommon to find two tenants presented for offences against each other in consecutive entries.

Fines might be acknowledgements of wrong-doing or heavy enough to discourage further offences. In 1650, a labourer might earn 1s per day,[40] so the 20s fine incurred by Thomas Kigell at Horton (Dorset) for putting his stock into the common field before the appointed time was a genuine punishment and not a token acknowledgement of an offence. In theory manor courts were restricted to levying fines up to 40s, thus in 1705 at Bamburgh (Northumberland), two tenants were fined 39s 11d each, one for getting the other arrested on a writ issued by the

---

37 Waddell, 'Governing England through the manor courts', 294-5.

38 Waddell, 'Governing England through the manor courts', 296-7.

39 French, 'Urban common rights', 41. French 'Urban agriculture, commons and commoners', 178.

40 Thorold Rogers, *Six centuries of work and wages*, 432.

Court of King's Bench and the other for indicting the first at the Quarter Sessions.[41] In some courts they could be higher.[42] However there are plenty of examples of fines being levied at higher levels and even written into the customs, like the £5 penalty imposed at Okeford Fitzpaine (Dorset) for removing cattle from the lord's pound (see section 9).

The Court Baron acted as a tribunal for the lord's tenants to bring private disputes against each other, using the machinery of the court to adjudicate on cases for a fee. Charges of trespass, debt or and breach of contract made between tenants comprised a substantial amount of business in late medieval manor courts, as lords had actively encouraged private litigation and profited from the fines imposed. This form of dispute resolution worked well when all tenants were resident within the manor and courts were held at regular intervals several times each year. By the sixteenth century, increasing numbers of absentee tenants, less frequent sittings of the Court Baron and competition from county and national courts resulted in

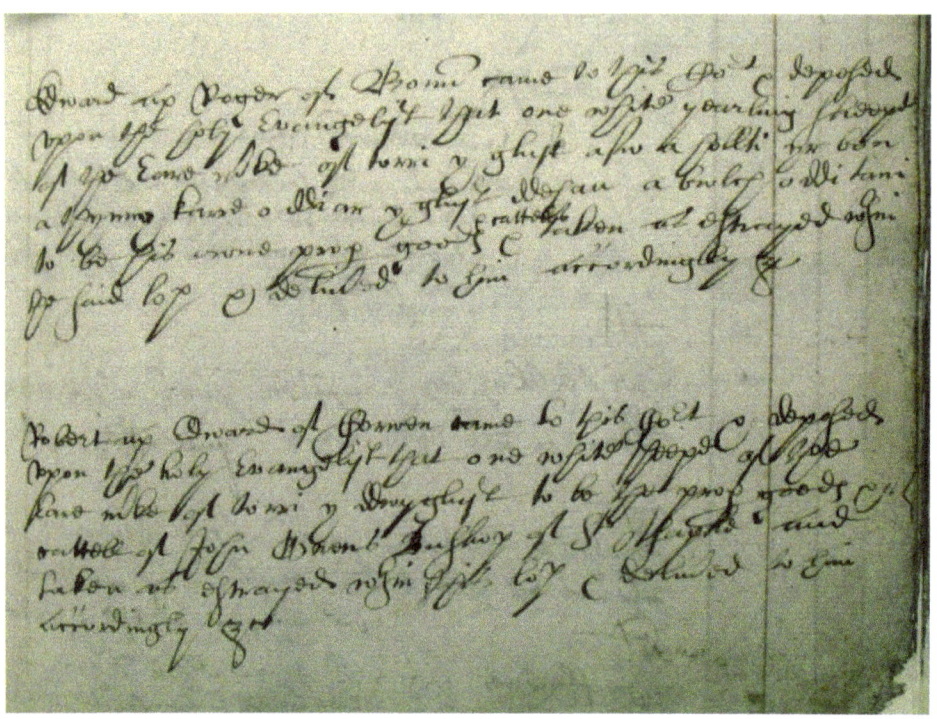

8. Glyndyfrdwy manor, Denbighshire, court book 1643-1665.
This court book contains small sections in Welsh, here describing the ear marks of stray sheep.

Edward ap Roger of Bonu[m] [Bonwm] *came to this Co[u]rt & deposed upon the holy Evangelist that one white yearling sheepe of the Eare m[ar]ke of torri y glust asw a hollti yr bon a thynny karre o ddi ar y glust ddehau a bwlch o ddi tani to be his owne prop[er] goodes & cattelys* [chattels] *& taken as estrayed w[it]hin the said lo[rdshi]p & deliv[er]ed to him accordingly etc*
Robert ap Edward of Corwen came to this Co[u]rt & deposed upon the holy Evangelist that one white sheepe of the Eare m[ar]ke of torri y ddwy glust to be the prop[er] goodes & cattell [chattels] *of John Owens Bushop of St Asaphe and taken as estrayed w[it]hin this lo[rdshi]p & deliv[er]ed to him accordingly etc.*

---
41 Webb and Webb, *English Local Government*, 91.

42 Waddell, 'Governing England through the manor courts', 288-9.

a gradual decline in cases of dispute resolution between tenants. This was even the case on a highly active royal manor, Havering (Essex), where private suits fell by three quarters between 1470 and 1564.[43] On the smaller manors, where courts were held only once a year or a couple of times in each decade, tenants found other courts to prosecute their private business and so the role of the manorial courts in local dispute resolution diminished or vanished completely. Nevertheless, on larger manors where the Court Baron was held more often, there might still be a substantial range of private litigation even into the eighteenth century.

A separate court of estrays, kept on several Welsh manors and elsewhere, determined the ownership of livestock pastured on common lands when disputes arose and returned stray animals to their rightful owners. This function was particularly important on manors with large areas of common pasture where animals were grazed for much of the year. The court at Denbigh survived well into the later twentieth century, producing various records even including photographs.

Although a lord might hold the courts of two manors together, they could remain distinct entities with separate customs. In Oxfordshire, the courts for Bloxham Beauchamp and Bloxham Fiennes, were held together in a single session, two juries were empanelled with several tenants who held land in both manors serving on both juries. Elsewhere a court might be held for two or three manors although some practical and administrative differences remained: at Mere (Wiltshire) the courts of the manors of Zeals Clevedon and Woodlands had been held together from around 1455 with those of Zeals Aylesbury added by 1532.[44] Separate rentals and surveys were compiled for all three manors until at least 1575 and during the seventeenth century the steward still had to refer back to the court rolls of each individual manor to establish their different customs relating to matters like the inheritance rights of widows.

Custom usually dictated that the court had to be held within the manor; in the eighteenth century, in Dorset, Beaminster Prima and Beaminster Secunda manors were owned by the same lord whose steward presided over his courts on the same day at the White Hart Hotel where the function room straddled the boundary between the two manors:

> The three Beaminster manors, or the lands comprising them, are much intermixed. No map of either manor exists, and there are no means of defining their boundaries. Some houses and fields are partly in one manor and partly in another. The White Hart Hotel is an instance of this, the archway forming the division between the manors. For many years prior to 1888 the half-yearly Manor Courts were held in this hotel, the steward and homage first assembling at the west end of the large room on the first floor to hold a court in and for Prima Manor, then proceeding to the other end to hold a court in and for Secunda, and finally dining together.[45]

The business of the post-medieval Court Baron declined everywhere until by the twentieth century the few remaining courts dealt almost exclusively with administration of copyhold tenancies. This was still an important role, as even in the nineteenth century copyhold formed a significant quantity of agricultural land

---

43 McIntosh, *A community transformed*, 297-317.

44 VCH Wilts, v.19, Mere hundred, forthcoming

45 Hine, *The History of Beaminster*, 257.

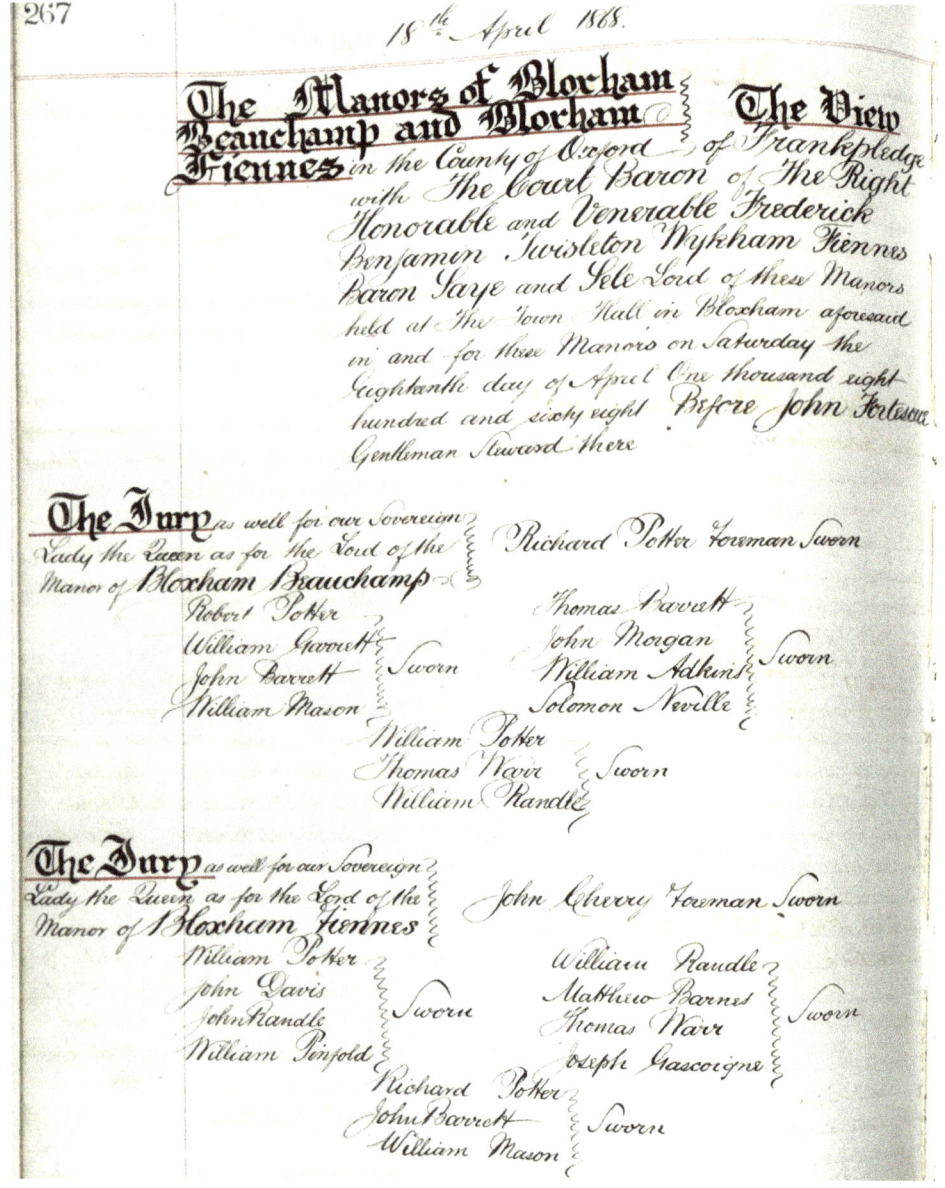

9. Bloxham Beauchamp and Bloxham Fiennes, Oxfordshire, 1868.
The heading names to lord of the manors and the steward, provides the location of the court and that it is styled a view of frankpledge with a Court Baron. The two courts were held together at the same session with juries empanelled for each court.

and the social and economic development of those communities, where it survived, cannot be understood without reference to its management. Similarly, the Court Baron's role in governance of communal resources, such as stocking commons, dividing meadow, preventing encroachment or maintaining hedges gave the tenants a direct input into their management which was lost when the court ceased to be held or when it ceased to regulate these areas. As with so many aspects of manorial history, the decline or abandonment of the Court Baron could happen centuries apart on adjacent manors.

Gradually the other business brought to the Court Baron diminished and it dealt almost exclusively with land transfers or the allied issues of applications for inheritances and guardianships, authorising forfeitures and re-allocations and occasional boundary disputes. This had occurred at Terling (Essex) by the sixteenth century and Wakefield (Yorkshire) by the mid-seventeenth century.[46] While the breadth of business was reduced to property related matters these remain of interest to social and economic historians as they include details of occupations, place names, the value of land (through rents and entry fines), inheritance patterns and even a few residual work services and rents in kind.

6
Tenants and Tenancies

The land that made up each manor might be held in several different ways. At the core of the manor the 'demesne' was a home farm managed directly by the lord or his officers, other land was held by tenants as freehold or as customary land, which by the sixteenth century was most commonly copyhold. Both demesne or customary land could be converted to leasehold by the lord of the manor, while freehold could be leased by the freeholder. Each type of landholding was present in different forms in different regions, changed in their nature over time, but not all were found on every manor. Administration of land was a mainstay of the Court Baron and at the core of the records maintained by the steward whose court rolls, rentals, accounts and surveys kept track of who held different pieces of land, the terms of their tenancies and the rents payable.

Among the tenants of the manor the medieval forms of land holding developed into the freehold, leasehold and copyhold tenancies common from the sixteenth century.[47] Not all forms of tenure were present on every manor or on the same estate. In 1622 on the St John estate, Glamorgan, the land at Penmark manor was divided 89% copyhold and leasehold, 10% freehold and 1% demesne, while at Fonmon manor there was 75% copyhold and leasehold, 4% freehold and 21% demesne, there was no demesne at Barry which had 89% copyhold and leasehold and 11% freehold, or at Llancadle 75% copyhold and leasehold and

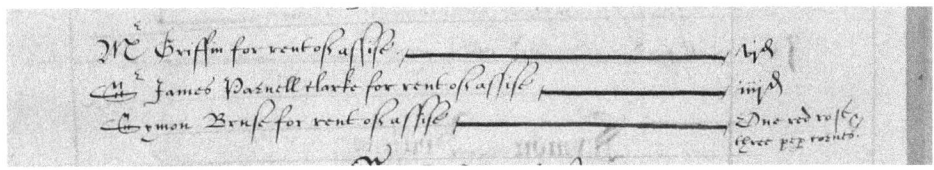

10. Gretton manor, Northamptonshire, 1587.
Mr Griffin for rent of assise. vjd
Sir James Parnell, clarke, for rent of assise iiijd
Symon Bruse for rent of assise One red rose & three pep[er] cornes.

---

46   Wrightson and Levine, *Poverty and piety in an English village*, 11-13. Fraser and Emsley, *Court rolls of the manor of Wakefield*, 1639-40, xiii-xvi.

47   Bailey, 'The transformation of customary tenures in southern England', 210-30.

25% freehold.[48] Across the England and Wales manors developed a mixture of tenancy arrangements and the same tenant might hold copyhold, leasehold and freehold as part of their portfolio.

Freeholders, despite the name, were still tenants of the lord of the manor and owed suit at (i.e. were obliged to attend) either his Court Baron or, more frequently, the Court Leet. Their land was usually held for a fixed rent paid in cash, or by a token such as a pepper corn or a red rose by which they recognised the superior status of the lord; the land was generally free from most customary obligations.[49] The cash rents were set when the freehold was granted, often in the 12th or 13th centuries, so their actual value diminished over time to a point where many became negligible and the least valuable land to the lord.[50] Freehold could be exchanged between individuals without reference to the manor court and from the earliest times disputes relating to freehold could be resolved in the higher courts. Although freeholders were able to dispose of their land at will each new tenant still acknowledged the lord of the manor through a fine called a 'relief' when they took possession. Both the rent and relief on freehold land was often fixed at a low level, so the properties became less valuable to the lord of the manor as the income was eroded by inflation. Freehold tenancies generally had few, if any, labour services, but they did have rights to place stock on common grazing and responsibilities to maintain infrastructure which occasionally brought the holder to the courts. Because many freeholders had multiple properties on different manors, which they could sub-let to under tenants without a licence from the lord of the manor, the obligation to attend the court could be ignored on payment of a small fine and they might never set foot on the manor.

Low rents, limited customary obligations and absentee status combined to limit the role played by freeholders in manorial administration. Consequently they appear in disproportionately low numbers in the court rolls and their presence is best observed through the entries for their lands in rentals and surveys.

Knights' fees were a sub-set of freeholds held by military service of up to 40 days per year owed by the lord of the manor to the Crown. Holders of knights' fees rarely actually carried out military service as an obligation after 1200, but they might be called upon to pay additional taxes. They were abolished as a form of tenure for manorial lords in 1666, but sometimes continued to be recorded in surveys of their tenants where freeholders had owed military service on behalf of the lord of the manor instead of paying a rent.

Customary tenancies developed from servile tenures. Tenants began to receive a written copy of the court record of land transactions around 1300, the earliest-known copy agreement, from Nywelond manor in Sherborne (Dorset), is dated 1306,[51] and written copies had become common by 1500.[52] By the sixteenth century local forms of hereditary customary tenure had developed across the country in parallel, gradually losing their associations with servile obligations, issuing copies of court roll, but not becoming a consistent form of tenancy. Customary tenants might owe some residual seasonal labour services, but these were mostly commuted for a cash sum before 1300, and they might owe some of their rents in kind, often

---

48   Griffiths, 'Manor court records and the historian: Penmark, Fonmon and Barry', 51-3.

49   Bailey, *The English manor*, 27-8.

50   Campbell, 'The agrarian problem in the early fourteenth century', 43-4.

51   This document is Dorset History Centre D-SHA/M1A, see Currie, 'Tenants' copies of court rolls' for a discussion of the early development of copies.

52   Bailey, 'The transformation of customary tenures in southern England', 220.

11. Monkton Up Wimborne manor, Dorset, 1657.
A presentment illustrating the complications that may arise from the division of a tenement. The freeholder did not have to seek permission to divide and sell a knight's fee, leaving the jury to struggle with the question of who owed the various obligations attached to it.

First, They present That John Budden, gen[tleman] was some tymes a Freeholder of this Mannor and hath done his Suite and Service to this Court in his life time (being now dead) passed away his Mannor or Farme of Hayrewood formerly and \now/ holden of this Mannor by a whole Knights Fee to his sonn Thomas Budden, who since sold it to Mr Bettsworth who likewise hath sold the same to Richard Low Esq[uire], Thomas Blanchard gent[leman] and to John Bampton in severall parcells therefore the Jurie desireth respite till the next Court to satisfye themselves what rent is due to the Lord of this Mannor from the p[er]sons aforesaid And what relieffe is or may be due upon the death or alienac[i]on of either of them and whether they are all to doe Suite and Service to the said Court or but one of them & which of them.

in the form of cocks and hens at winter feast days. They frequently paid a heriot, or death duty, of the best animal on their tenement and a fixed rent which, like the freeholders' rents, was originally set at a market rent but gradually reduced in real value over time. Incoming tenants paid an entry fine which was fixed on some manors and variable on others. All customary tenants were obliged to attend the manor court whenever it was held and to serve as officers of the court, receiving rights to the use of common assets in return.

By the end of the fifteenth century, the various customary tenures had gradually evolved into a form of tenancy known as copyhold which was recognised by stewards and lawyers as a distinct form of tenure. Like their medieval predecessors copyholds could still only be granted, exchanged or surrendered in the manor court, and throughout the fourteenth and fifteenth centuries disputes between tenants and landlord regarding customary tenancies were brought exclusively to

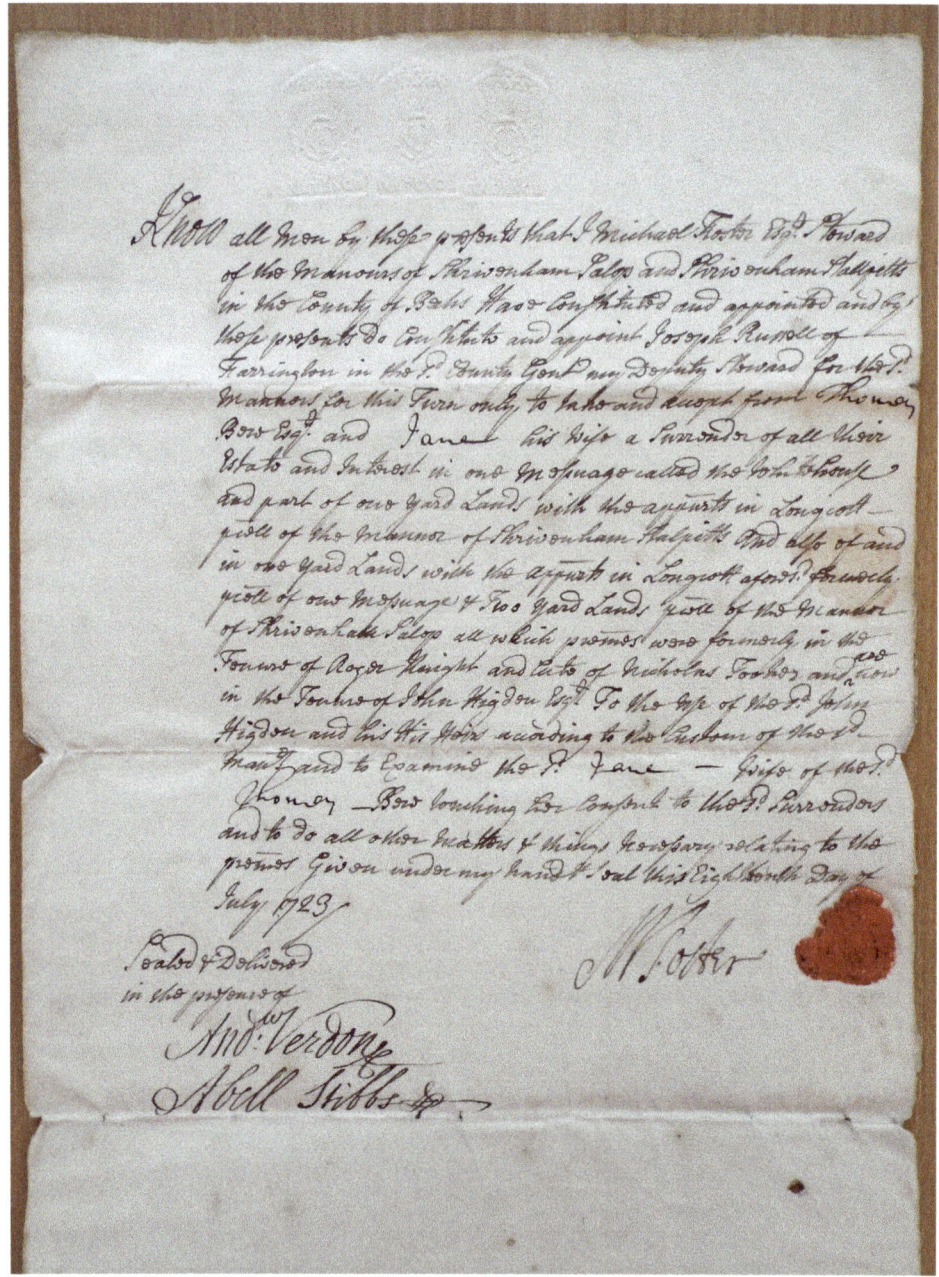

the manorial courts, but legal disputes relating to copyhold could be heard in Chancery and the higher courts.[53] The administration of these copyhold tenancies remained one of the principal functions of the manor court until their abolition in the twentieth century.

A simplified process of the transfer of copyhold land operated as follows. First, the land would come into the hands of the lord, either through a surrender

---

53   Garnett-Goodyear, 'Common law and the manor courts', 35-51.

12. *(opposite page)* Shrivenham Stalpitts, Berkshire, 1723.
A surrender of copyhold to the use of another tenant:
Know all Men by these presents that I Michael Foster Esq[uir]e Steward of the Manours of Shrivenham Salop and Shrivenham Stallpitts in the County Berks Have Constituted and appointed and by these presents do Constitute and appoint Joseph Russell of Farrington in the s[ai]d County Gent[leman] my Deputy Steward for the s[ai]d Mannors for this Turn only to take and accept from Thomas Bere Esq[uir]e and Jane his Wife a Surrender of all their Estate and Interest in one Messuage called the Whitehouse and part of one Yard Lands with the appurt[enance]s in Longcott p[ar]cell of the Mannor of Shrivenham Stalpitts And also of and in one Yard Lands with the appurt[enance]s in Longcott afores[ai]d formerly p[ar]cell of one Messuage & Two Yard Lands p[ar]cell of the Mannor of Shrivenham Salop all which prem[is]es were formerly in the Tenure of Roger Knight and late of Nicholas xxx and \are/ now in the Tenure of John Higden Esq[uir]e To the use of the s[ai]d John Higden and his ~~His~~ Heirs according to the Custom of the s[ai]d Man[ou]r and to Examine the s[ai]d Jane Wife of the s[ai]d Thomas Bere touching her Consent to the s[ai]d Surrenders and to do all other Matters & things Necessary relating to the prem[is]es Given under my hand & seal this Eighteenth Day of July 1723.

made by the current tenant, by death or by forfeit, then the lord or his steward would re-grant the land to another tenant. The surrender could be made in court, or out of court in the presence of witnesses, sometimes a 'surrender to use'. When a copyhold was surrendered directly to another tenant in what amounted to a sale, that action would later be ratified at the Court Baron. When a tenant died, or the copyhold was forfeit for poor maintenance, the heir could come forward and make a claim; if no heirs came forward, the copyhold escheated (passed back) to the lord who might re-grant it to another tenant. At this stage, the lord might have the opportunity to change its status to leasehold or freehold or to add it to his own directly managed lands. As it was generally established by the seventeenth century that new copyhold land could not be created when copyholds were converted or taken in hand their overall number reduced.[54] In the nineteenth century the creation of new copyholds from waste was considered, and Parliament could create replacement copyhold by enclosure acts, but private creation of copyhold by enclosure of commons was specifically prohibited under the Copyhold Act 1887.[55] When a copyhold was granted to a new tenant, a new copyhold agreement was drawn up, known as an admission, and in the most straightforward cases, the surrender and admission were recorded in the same document. In an echo of the early medieval relationship between lord and tenant, the new tenant swore fealty to the lord and might hold or kiss the steward's staff of office to enact a physical transfer through the object that carried the lord's authority. The steward recorded the transaction in the court roll and the tenant received a parchment copy of the copyhold agreement.

Where copyhold was hereditary, the incoming tenant had to demonstrate that they were the next heir, according to the customs of the manor, to secure their admittance. This might involve the decision of the jury if the inheritance was from a distant relative or if there were counter claims by children of second and third marriages. Where the copyhold was held for lives, the term was determined by the lifetimes of named lives on the copy at the last admission. A tenant would come to the manor court and take on a property for the term of his own life and the lives of two close relatives, usually siblings or children. Sometimes, tenants would wait for all three lives to expire before renewing the copyhold as, by custom, their heir would usually be allowed to take out a new copyhold. However, when all three named tenants had died there was always the chance that the lord might take the land into his own hands or grant it to another tenant, so additional lives could be

---

54 Harvey, *Manorial Records*, 57-8.

55 Jessel, *Law of the manor*, 88-91.

added, on payment of a fine to the lord, on the death of the first or second life.

When a copyhold was issued for a term of lives an entry fine was payable to the lord each time a new name or names were added. For copyholds of inheritance a fine was payable when it passed from one tenant to another. In both cases widows of incumbent tenants were usually allowed to occupy the tenement during their widowhood if they did not remarry, or lived 'sole and chaste', although on some manors were copyholders were issued for terms of lives only the widow of the first named tenant had this right. In most places the entry fines, payable when a new name was added to the copyhold, were set by the steward and could be increased, while the rents of copyholds were set by custom and remained fixed. Therefore, on many manors, a tenement that had a rent of 10s in 1400 still paid 10s rent in 1800, but whereas in 1400 the entry fine might also have been 10s by 1800 it might be £1,000. This was not always the case, on some East Anglian manors, and probably elsewhere, where entry fines had been high in the fourteenth century they remained fixed at a high level throughout the fifteenth century and became fixed by custom in the sixteenth century at the same rates that they had been charged 200 years previously.[56] On those copyhold which owed heriots they were usually payable on the death of male tenants, sometimes deferred during the life of a surviving widow and often remitted for poorer tenants.

Hereditary copyhold was common eastern England as well as parts of Cheshire, Lancashire and Somerset, and that that copyhold for a defined number of lives, usually three, was most common in the west.[57] Copyhold for terms of years was rare; Kerridge found that in the Midlands, where the incidence was highest, that the term was usually 21 years, but could be as high as 60, or as low as nine. Whether a copyhold was hereditary or held for terms of years or lives it was held according to the customs of the manor, such as those relating to the rights of widows. On the manor of Portland (Dorset), copyhold of inheritance had a customary variation called 'church gift' recorded in a survey of 1650:

> by Custom allso any Tennant Houlding his Lands and Tenements of the said Mannor, may at the parish Church of Portland in the presence of two or more witnesses surrender his Estate or any part thereof unto any person whatsoever.[58]

The copy of court roll usually includes the date on which the court was held, the names of the lord of the manor and/or the steward, the name of the tenant who had come to court to gain admission to the property, a description of the lands that were to be transferred, the terms upon which the land was to be held including the length of the agreement, and a statement that the tenant had sworn fealty to the lord of the manor. The amount of detail provided by these copies varies over time and between manors. The property may have a detailed description by reference to fixed points in the landscape, roads and field boundaries; it may be located by the names of adjacent tenants; or identified by a former tenant and given an estimated acreage.

An example of the conditions and progress of a copyhold tenure might run as follows: John Smith is the initial life on the copyhold and recipient of the property. He is admitted for the term of his own life and the lives of his two children, Richard and Robert. On most manors, a heriot would be payable

---

56 Whittle, *Development of agrarian capitalism*, 79-81.

57 Kerridge, *Agrarian problems*, 35-8.

58 Bettey, '"Ancient custom time out of mind", copyhold tenure in the west country', 309.

on John's death, and his widow would have the right to continue to occupy the property unless she remarried. On the death of John and his widow, the property would pass to Richard, unless he too had died, in which case it would pass to Robert or to Richard's heir. It is important to note that the named lives were not necessarily the heirs to the property. If Richard had died, his children had the right to inherit despite their uncle Robert's name being on the copyhold. Richard's children would be admitted to the land, but only for the term of Robert's lifetime, because the copyhold defined the length of the tenure and not the next heir. When each tenant died, the remaining named tenants and their heirs could come to the court and add another name to the copyhold on payment of a fine, as noted above, but if the last named tenant died, it would pass back into the hands of the lord of the manor who would have the opportunity to retain it as

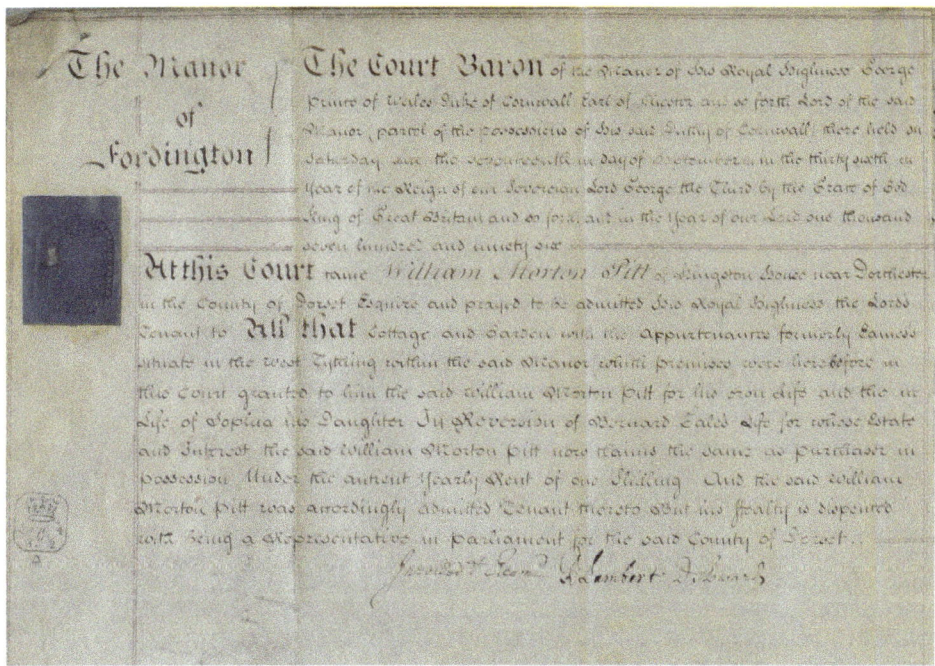

13. Fordington, Dorset, 1796.
A copy of court roll granting William Morton Pitt admittance to customary land. This document clearly illustrates how far customary tenure had moved from its medieval origins as the form of holding for unfree peasants. The lord was the Prince of Wales, so clearly not present at the court, and the tenant, as a member of Parliament, had his fealty to the lord waived.

At this Court came William Morton Pitt of Kingston House near Dorchester in the county of Dorset Esquire and prayed to be admitted His Royal Highness the Lord's tenant to all that Cottage and Garden with the Appurtenances formerly Eames's situate in the West Tything within the said Manor (which premises were herebefore in the Court granted to him the said William Morton Pitt for his own Life and the Life of Sophia his Daughter In Reversion of Bernard Gale's Life for whose Estate and Interest the said William Morton Pitt now claims the same as Purchaser in possession Under the ancient Yearly Rent of one Shilling And the said William Morton Pitt was accordingly admitted Tenant thereto But his Fealty is dispenced with being a Representative in Parliament for the said County of Dorset.

part of his own land or to admit a new tenant.

Thomas Hardy's fictional character, Giles Winterborne, in *The Woodlanders* expresses both the sense of security that tenants gained from their copyholds and provides an example of the complex arrangements of tenure for lives that continued when they were replaced by leases for lives. Winterborne

> *marvelled what people could have been thinking about in the past to invent such precarious tenures as these; still more, what could have induced his ancestors at Hintock, and other village people, to exchange their old copyholds for life-leases. ... They were ordinary leases for three lives, which a member of the South family, some fifty years before this time, had accepted of the lord of the manor in lieu of certain copyholds and other rights, in consideration of having the dilapidated houses rebuilt by said lord. They had come into his father's possession chiefly through his mother, who was a South.*

Giles Winterborne held the property during the life of John South, whose life was the last of three lives that set the term of the lease, but it passed through a different line of inheritance.

For manorial lords, the conversion of copyhold to leasehold had the advantage of creating a predictable and fixed rent recalculated at market value with each renewal. Entry fines were sometimes retained, but overall the fines and rents were spread more evenly over the period of the lease. A further reason for conversion might be that elderly tenants engaged in sham marriages with the intention of evading high entry fines. Bettey cites several examples of these intergenerational marriages in Dorset, Somerset and Wiltshire and they were common enough for stewards to use these precedents as a reason to convert the tenure. One such from Kilmersdon (Somerset) in 1674 is contained in a letter from Gabriel Goodman, the lord of the manor, to his steward requesting that he granted no more copyholds, but to insist on leases for term of years which would not be subject to custom of the manor. This was because of the abuse of widows' estate, and he gives an example of a copyhold tenant named Maggs who was "86 or 88 years of age and a very Infirme man" who, on his deathbed, had married his maidservant.[59]

A suggestion to convert copyholds to freehold made during the Commonwealth never gained much support; it would have required considerable compensation payments to lords, and, while freehold would appear to be the most attractive form of tenure to which a customary tenant might aspire, the lack of customary rights meant that there was also opposition from copyholders.[60]

In the nineteenth century, copyholds began to be converted into freeholds as well as leaseholds by means of conveyances of the fee simple from lord to tenant. This process was facilitated by the purchase by the copyholder of a deed of enfranchisement from the lord of the manor and when the 1852 Copyhold Act enabled any copyholder to demand a deed of enfranchisement,[61] it became common even where lords had previously resisted the change. The provisions of Copyhold Acts of 1841, 1843, 1844, 1852, 1858 and 1887 were consolidated in an Act of 1894,[62] and most copyhold had already been converted by its final abolition under the Act of 1922. Deeds of enfranchisement, as with copyholds, are found in

---

59   Bettey, '"Ancient custom time out of mind", copyhold tenure in the west country', 319-20.

60   Brooks, 'The agrarian problem in revolutionary England', 192-4.

61   Copyhold Act 1852 (15 & 16 Vict. c.51).

62   Copyhold Act 1894 (56 & 57 Vict. c.46).

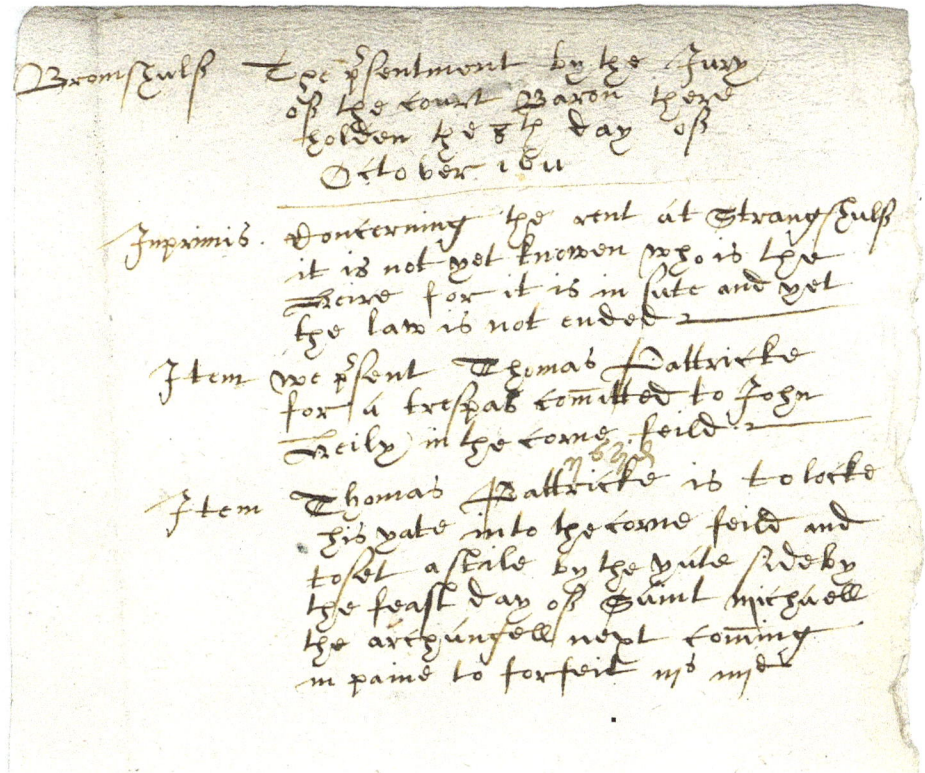

14. Bromshulf [Bramshall] manor, Staffordshire, 1611.
The first presentment notes that a matter of inheritance can not be resolved until a higher court adjudication has been made.
Note also the use of the character 'yogh', 3, here representing a hard 'gh' or 'g'.

Bromshulf	The p[re]sentment by the Jury
	of the Court Baron there
	holden the 8th day of
	October 1611
Inprimis [Firstly]	Concerning the rent at Strangshulf
	it is not yet knowen who is the
	Heire for it is in sute ond yet
	the law is not ended.
Item,	We p[re]sent Thomas Pattricke
	for a trespas com[m]itted to John
	Heily in the corne field.
Item,	Thomas Pattricke \ ijs. vjd. / is to locke
	his 3ate into the corne field and
	to set a stile by the 3ate side by
	the feast day of Saint Michaell
	the archangell next com[m]ing
	in paine to forfeit iijs. iiijd.

family and estate collections in county archives and in several series in The National Archives, particularly MAF 9 and MAF 20. There appears to be a varied survival rate for these records in different counties, in Dorset and Somerset there are only two dozen manors with enfranchisement documents in these classes, although enfranchisement is known to have taken place in others, whereas for Norfolk and

Suffolk there are documents for more than four hundred manors in each county. That enfranchisement of copyhold took place in so many of these East Anglian manors demonstrates its widespread survival, at least in this part of the country and perhaps elsewhere, into the second half of the nineteenth century.

Copyhold tenure was the principal reason for the survival of the Court Baron beyond the eighteenth century, in some places even beyond the sixteenth century. It was a form of tenure that could only be conveyed at the Court Baron and copyhold tenants made up the mainstay of the courts jurors, officers and homage.

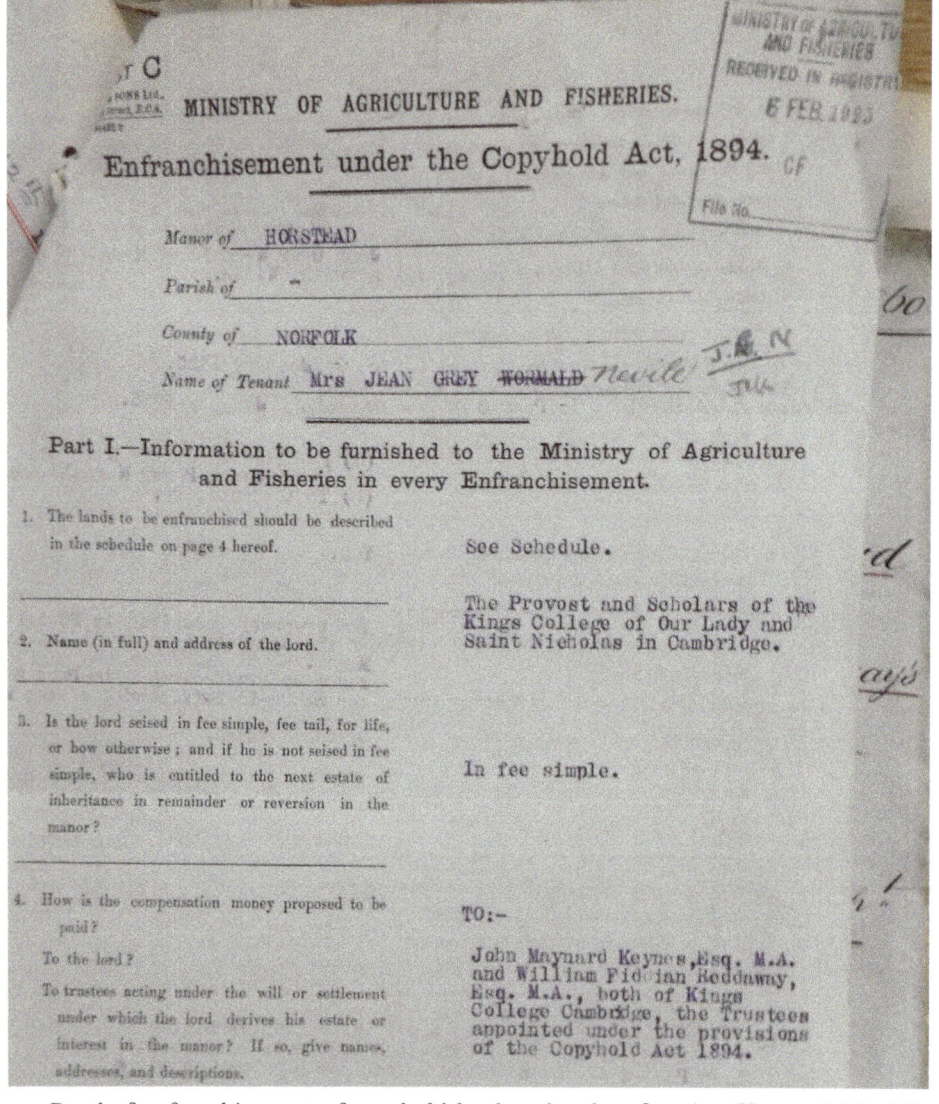

15. Deed of enfranchisement of copyhold land under the 1894 Act, Horstead, Norfolk, 1923.

In the sixteenth century, there was an active land market among peasants involving copyhold land; in many places, particularly East Anglia, traditional customary tenements had broken up. Elsewhere, the traditional land units survived, but were brought together into larger holdings, and increasingly copyhold was exchanged and sub-let by people who were not resident on the manor. Dyer's study of manors in the West Midlands captures this period of transition; holdings could still be declared forfeit if tenants did not live on the land and combined holdings were broken up at the death of the tenant in the mid-fifteenth century, but by the start of the sixteenth century, larger holdings were brought together and passed intact between generations and copyholds were purchased by merchants and gentlemen.[63] Across the country over succeeding generations, the combination of larger holdings, non-resident tenants and sub-letting eventually led to there being insufficient numbers of resident tenants with an interest in the community to serve as officers and to use the manorial court as a regular forum for regulation.

Copies of court roll, surrenders and admissions are records of title and are not considered to be manorial documents under the specific terms of the Manorial Documents Rules; therefore, they are not included in the Manorial Documents Register. Nevertheless, they are some of the most numerous documents surviving from manorial administrations in county archives, providing detailed evidence of individual holdings, which may be added together to give an idea of the structure of those manors where no court rolls, rentals or surveys have survived.

Three regions: Wales, northern England and Cornwall, had their own distinct forms of customary tenure that were sufficiently different from copyhold to be classed as separate forms of tenancy.[64] In Wales, some freeholds had been created from customary land and retained some customary rights and obligations in a fusion of the two forms. A Cornish 'conventionary' tenure was hereditary and owed various customary obligations, it was granted on seven year leases renewed every seven years at a court of assession. A form of tenure called 'tenant right', common in Durham, Northumberland, Cumberland, Westmorland and parts of Yorkshire, was a form of customary leasehold. It was an hereditary tenure at the wishes of the tenant, without interference from the lord, and carried an obligation to perform military service.[65] Tenant right was abolished in 1603, but it took a further generation for landlords and tenants to negotiate a replacement tenure.

Leasehold, for a term of years or a hereditary tenure for one, two or three lives, might consist of former freehold, customary or demesne land. Commonly from the middle of the fourteenth century, the whole of the demesne was leased to a 'farmer' often for a term of 21 years for a cash rent, and other assets such as mills and warrens could be leased on similar terms. Population decline from the fourteenth century resulted in areas where there were a large number of vacant tenements and the more profitable arable or meadow might be separated out and leased for a short period of a year or a season. All customary land was held 'at will of the lord', copyhold usually being described as 'at the will of the lord by the customs of the manor', while customary land leased for short periods might just be described as held 'at will'. Land leased 'at will' for short periods, often for a year or a season, was granted without security for a simple cash rent and might consist of parts of vacant tenements, sections of the demesne or land newly brought into cultivation from waste. As well as these parcels of land whole tenements that had been held in villeinage could be converted to customary leasehold held for terms of lives or years.[66] Leaseholders paid an entry fine, a market rent fixed at the start of the lease

---

63 Dyer, 'Peasant holdings in West Midlands villages', 277-94.

64 Kerridge, *Agrarian problems in the sixteenth century and after*, 41-4.

65 Morrin, 'Transfer of leasehold on Durham cathedral estate', 119-32.

66 Bailey, *The English manor*, 36-7.

and sometimes a heriot when one was owed on the land according to the terms of its tenure before it became leasehold. When leasing land enclosed from the waste in Lancashire, some estates preferred a shorter term of ten years, others allowed leases of up to 100 years but a standard term of 21 years was common.[67] Unlike copyhold, when leases were granted for terms of lives there was no presumption that additional lives may be added and the levels of the entry fines and rents could be reset at each new lease.

Leaseholders were usually resident on the manor and more likely to participate in the court rolls than the freeholders. However, they did not always have the same long term interest in the land as customary tenants. They were more likely to be incomers into a manor, and more likely to move away as their leases expired. Nor were they always obliged to serve in the same offices as the customary tenants or to attend the manorial court.

Conversion of demesnes and customary land to leasehold happened over a long period, usually weakening the structure of the manor and the authority of the Court Baron. At Birdbrook (Essex) in the later fourteenth century, customary tenure of standard holdings was abandoned in favour of leaseholds.[68] Schofield suggests that at Birdbrook the introduction of leaseholders from outside the manor was both the symptom and the cause of a weakened manorial structure and this directly resulted in a reduction in the authority of the manor court as the voice of peasant custom.[69] Elsewhere in Essex at Earls Colne in the first half of the seventeenth century, a substantial block of demesne land was broken up and issued in 75 leases, over two generations of lordship by the Harkenden family, on short term leases mostly for seven years or less.[70] Here, the short term nature of the leases reflects a pool of tenants who moved on from one tenancy to another rather than families with copyholds acquiring and releasing additional land as their households expanded and contracted. Again the introduction of leasehold was seen to weaken the structure of the manor and the authority of the manor court.

Much of the interest in the late medieval and post medieval manor revolves around the development of new tenancies, the survival of archaic processes in some places and the adoption of new terms and conditions in others. On those manors where an active peasant land market developed in the fifteenth century land was bought and sold by the acre, while in those with a less active market the traditional customary units such as virgates, yardlands, bovates, and oxgangs were retained and survived into the seventeenth and eighteenth centuries.[71] The break up of demesnes and development of copyhold tenure and its subsequent conversion to leasehold and freehold were parts of a process which which began in the thirteenth century and concluded in the twentieth century with substantial local and regional variation.

---

67 Shannon, 'Risks and rewards of wasteland enclosure', 157-8.

68 Schofield, 'The late medieval view of frankpledge and the tithing system', 414.

69 Schofield, 'The late medieval view of frankpledge and the tithing system', 435-9.

70 French and Hoyle, '*English Individualism* refuted: and reasserted', 619.

71 Whittle and Yates, '"Pays reel" ou "pays legal"?: Contrasting patterns of land tenure and social structure', 1-26.

7
The Court Leet

The Court Leet was held as a franchise from the Crown by a lord of one of the manors within the vill or by other institutions. Most leets had been 'privatised' in this way by the mid thirteenth century, so by the early modern period they were treated in effect as seigniorial courts.[72] However, those required to attend the leet were drawn from a wider group than the manorial tenants required to attend the Court Baron, and their business, too, was distinct. The leet was associated with the view of frankpledge, which required all males over the age of 12 within a defined geographical area (usually the vill, which was the lowest unit of civil government roughly coterminous with the parish) to be sworn into groups which provided surety for each other. The representatives of a collection of tithings, known as tithingmen, met once or twice each year, almost always in late September or October shortly after Michaelmas and sometimes in late March or April around Lady Day (25 March) or Hockday (the second Tuesday after Easter). The view of frankpledge was not only held by courts leet, but might instead be attached to a hundred or borough court. The tithings were theoretically comprised of groups of ten or twelve men, but many were much larger and, although they originated as groups of individuals, by the sixteenth century they were often associated with a particular set of tenements or a settlement. The members of a tithing were tasked with a range of issues including the apprehension of felons, dealing with local nuisances, investigating cases of bloodshed and reporting non-standard weights and measures.

Where the view of frankpledge was attached to the hundred court, no Court Leet was held, or a patchwork of courts might deal with the same business. In east Dorset, the view of frankpledge for the Badbury Hundred court was attended by the representatives of 11 tithings, while those for four other tithings went to the Court Leet attached to the manor of Kingston Lacy, within the same hundred. Only customary tenants were obliged to attend every session of the Court Baron, but many freeholders were obliged to attend the Court Leet. The obligation of tenants to attend the Court Leet was a significant factor in the decision of some lords to continue holding their Court Baron in the seventeenth and eighteenth centuries as it increased the range of business, ensured higher attendance and justified maintaining the administration.

On larger manors the leet might be divided between different townships. Wakefield manor (Yorkshire) had a single Court Baron held at Wakefield every three

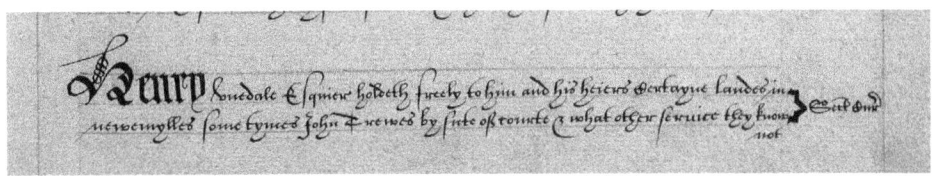

16. Langton Wallis, Dorset, 1585

Henry Uvedale Esquier freely to him and his heiers Certayne Landes in   } *sec[ta] cur[ia]*
newemylles sometymes John Trewes by sute of courte & what other service they know not}

---

72   Jewell, *English Local administration in the middle ages*, 50, 162-5.

weeks, but the courts leet were held at Wakefield on the Saturdays after Michaelmas and Easter, at Halifax on the following Monday, Brighouse in Hipperholme on the Tuesday and Kirkburton on the Wednesday.[73]

At the Court Leet, officers discharged the responsibilities of the Crown at a local level such as tithingmen and constables, who were appointed for the general maintenance of good order and played a role in securing infrastructure including highway and bridge maintenance. A second group of officers had specific areas of responsibility: ale-conners enforced the assize of ale; carniters and bread weighers controlled quality of meat and weights and measures of loaves; tanned hides were assessed for quality by scrutineers; chimney peepers made sure that chimneys were swept; scavengers kept refuse off the streets and scoured the drains. Not all of these officers were present in every leet and some leets had other specialist roles particular to their areas.

Minor disputes involving verbal abuse, assaults and nuisance were tried at this court, sometimes with the weapons used in fights being valued. Women appear frequently as scolds and gossips and this is one of the few areas of manorial court business where their appearances often out number those of men. With the responsibility for public order came the maintenance of stocks, ducking stools and bridewells and proclamations were made about public order offences such as harbouring strangers or gambling on dice and cards. The court decided if the hue and cry had been raised with justification and delegated other manorial or parish officers to assist the constables. When cases were deemed too serious to be tried at the Court Leet, they were referred upwards to the Justices of the Peace and Quarter Sessions.

The tithingmen collected payments of the hundred penny sometimes called *head silver*, *certum* or *cert money* which was paid at the Court Leet. Originally based on a penny per head of the adult male residents within the tithing, by the sixteenth century this was usually a fixed sum, and is sometimes known as the 'common fine'. The tithingmen also played a role in the collection of taxes for the Crown, including Lay Subsidies, and in musters of the militia, and while these roles are not usually recorded in the business of the leet, they are occasionally mentioned.

The Court Leet became much reduced in its responsibilities and functions from the middle of the sixteenth century due to a series of administrative reforms by central government. The Court Baron had responsibility for oversight of footpaths, droves and by-ways, but the King's Highways and significant bridges originally fell within the orbit of the Leet. Maintenance of highways began to pass from the manor to the parish with the Highways Act of 1555,[74] when the first of a series of highways acts provided for nominated parish surveyors of roads. Elizabethan Poor Law acts passed between 1552 and 1601 started a process by which parish officers including churchwardens and overseers of the poor gained responsibility for poor relief, apprenticeships and basic sanitation which subsequently grew into the provision of workhouses.[75] This process was gradual; at Standon manor (Hertfordshire) it was not unusual to record presentments relating to highways and the harbouring of vagrants well into the eighteenth century. Parliament explicitly directed that

---

73   Fraser and Emsley, *Court rolls of the manor of Wakefield*, 1639-40, xvi.

74   The Highways Act 1555 (2 & 3 Ph. and Mary, c.8).

75   The Act for the Provision and Relief of the Poor 1552 (5 & 6 Edw. VI, c.2) for the first time created a parish officer with the responsibility to collect alms, this Act and further Acts of 1555, 1563, 1572, 1575 and 1598 were brought together in The Poor Relief Act 1601 (43 Eliz. I, c.2).

the Turnpike Act of 1727 should be read in every Court Leet.[76] At Gillingham (Dorset), for much of the sixteenth, seventeenth and eighteenth centuries, officers of the Court Leet worked alongside those of the parish vestry and the Court Baron according to agreements established locally to solve problems and improve infrastructure within their communities.

The timescale of decline for the Court Leet was perhaps more varied than the Court Baron. Certainly some courts, such as those at Terling (Essex), had been abandoned by the end of the sixteenth century and disputes were taken to the Quarter Sessions.[77] However, this was by no means always the case. McIntosh found that in the sixteenth century the jurors at some courts leet were dealing with certain punishments and prosecuting offences that were largely ignored by higher courts.[78] The use of stocks, tumbrels and pillories and the prosecution of offences such as scolding and sheltering strangers were areas in which the Courts Leet acted in advance of national guidance. Waddell found that enforcement of the King's Peace and prosecution of marketing offences declined in the first half of the seventeenth century in Courts Leet generally, but in those that remained active presentments for general nuisances and repairs to infrastructure actually increased during the eighteenth century and were still made into the nineteenth century.[79] At Earls Colne, the majority of the business related to agrarian nuisances in the 1570s and 1580s, however falling attendances and an increase in the powers of parish officers meant that the court gave way to the parish vestry early in the following century.[80] At Brinkworth (Wiltshire) in the 1640s the business of the Court Leet was sufficiently varied as to include: regulation of brewers and butchers, appointments of tithingmen and constables, repairs to the King's highways, receiving the oath of allegiance, and harbouring strangers and relatives for whom the residents could not provide security, besides the business of the Court Baron which was held at the same sessions.[81] Most of the larger Court Leets were abolished under the Municipal Corporations Act 1835, when towns such as Manchester, which had used its Court Leet to administer the rapidly growing and industrialising city (with limited success) adopted a wholly new administration.[82] Others were retained as local regulatory authorities until the Administration of Justice Act 1977 brought about a general abolition for all but thirty-four named courts.

Market courts were held in some manors separate to the Court Leet to oversee those matters that related specifically to trade. Around 2,400 market charters and rights to hold fairs were granted to the lords of manors in the twelfth and thirteenth centuries.[83] Most of these had lapsed by the sixteenth century and markets that were held after 1500 were more likely to be administered by boroughs.

---

76   Webb and Webb, *English Local Government*, 118. An Act for punishing such Persons as shall wilfully and maliciously pull down or destroy Turnpikes for repairing Highways, or Locks or other Works, erected by Authority of Parliament, for making Rivers navigable (1 Geo. II, c.19).

77   Wrightson and Levine, *Poverty and piety in an English village*, 11-13.

78   McIntosh, *Controlling misbehaviour in England*, 39-40.

79   Waddell, 'Governing England through the manor courts', 302-7.

80   French and Hoyle, *The character of English rural society*, 167-71.

81   Crowley, *Court records of Brinkworth and Charlton*, 223-42.

82   The Municipal Corporations Act 1835 (5 & 6 Wm. IV, c.76).

83   The Centre for Metropolitan History, *Gazetteer of Markets and Fairs in England and Wales to 1516*, https://archives.history.ac.uk/gazetteer/gazweb2.html

Some still came under the authority of a manor court and where this was the case, the steward either gave the market a section of its own within the records of the Court Leet or Court Baron or kept a separate series of court rolls. For example, at Grishaugh manor (Norfolk), a separate market court book was maintained for the whole of the sixteenth century. The market courts accounted for tolls, recorded rents on stalls and shambles, oversaw regulations relating to weights and measures and appointed officers to oversee the market.

8
Stewards and Officers of the Courts

Manorial lords very rarely presided over their courts in person, in most cases a steward was appointed to hold the manor court and act on behalf of the lord. As mentioned above, the lord's authority might be physically transferred through a staff or rod of office which the steward held when granting property or making proclamations. In the sixteenth century, estates frequently appointed the younger sons of local gentry families, perhaps with some legal training, who, by the eighteenth and nineteenth centuries, gradually gave way to solicitors being employed. In 1809, on the death of his brother-in-law John Adey, a solicitor at Aylsham (Norfolk), the landscape gardener Humphry Repton wrote to John Wodehouse and William Wyndham to request that his son, William Repton, who was a partner in Adey's business, be appointed as steward to their manors where courts had formerly been held by Adey.[84] Wyndham's response was positive, but Wodehouse preferred to appoint a man who already managed several of his other manors.

Manorial stewards wrote documents intended to be used by themselves, their subordinates and their successors. Some of these documents, particularly court rolls, were produced according to legal standards and intended to be accessible for future generations as active works of reference. Technical legal, agricultural and procedural terms were used for precision. Many of these are unfamiliar to the modern reader and although those that had been adopted in the medieval period often changed their meaning on different manors over the centuries, the repetitive nature of the court's business means that the handwriting and terminology soon become familiar. Some manorial documents such as court rolls, custumals,

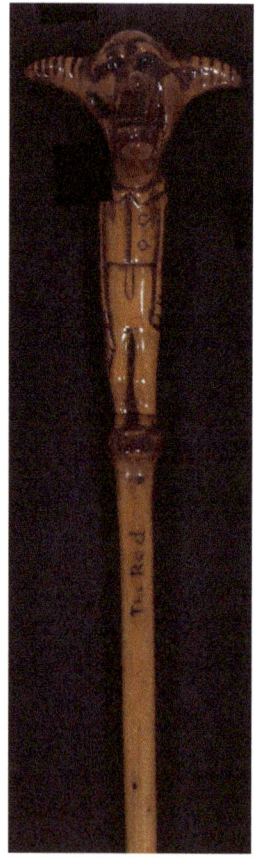

17. Little Aston alias Church Aston, Shropshire.
Steward's rod of office used to represent the authority of the lord of the manor in the century prior to the termination of manorial tenures in 1926.

---

84   Falvey, *Humphry Repton and his family*, 179-80 and 191-3.

presentments, perambulations and certain steward's papers were peculiar to the manor and were only ever produced by a manorial administration, while accounts, rentals, surveys and maps might be drawn up by an estate administrator and the distinction between manorial and estate documents is not always clear.

Stewards were assisted by written primers and exemplars which provided standard formats for recording the business of the courts. There had been medieval guides to estate management described by P. D. A. Harvey in his guide to *Manorial Records*,[85] all of which were referenced by later guides and all have modern editions. An anonymous treatise providing guidance for keeping courts, which was

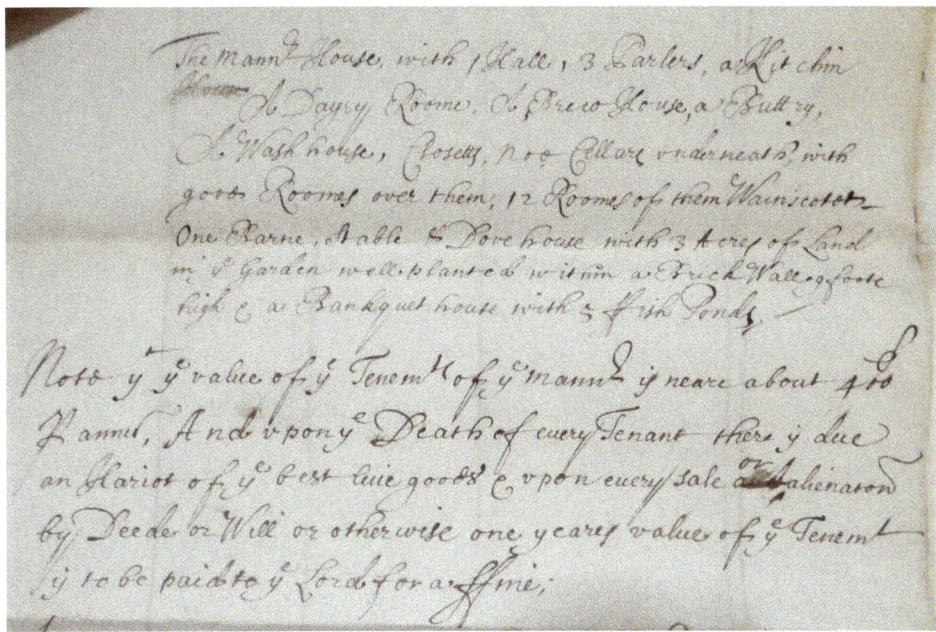

18. Great Stanmore Middlesex, 1674.
Steward's notes relating to the contents of the manor house when leased, the value of the manor and customs of the manor.
The Mann[ou]r House, with 1 Hall, 3 Parlers, a Kitchin House A Dayry Roome, A Brew House, a Buttry, A Wash house, Closetts, Noe Cellar[e]s underneath, with good Roomes over them, 12 Roomes of them Wainscoted. One Barne, Stable & Dove house with 3 Acres of Land in the Garden well planted within a Brick Wall 9 foote high & a Bankquet house with 5 Fish Ponds.
Note that the value of the Tenem[en]ts of the Mann[ou]r is neare about £400 Per annu[m], And upon the Death of every Tenant there is due an Hariot of the best live goods & upon every sale \or/ and alienac[i]on by Deede or Will or otherwise one yeares value of the Tenem[en]t is to be paid to the Lord for a Fine.

the first to appear in printed form, was published in 1510 ran to twenty editions by 1650. As noted above, Sir Edward Coke's *Compleate Copyholder* was first published in 1641. The most popular, Giles Jacob's *Compleat Court-Keeper* first published in 1713, contained a summary of statute law relating to the manor, with later editions including instructions relating to the enfranchisement of copyhold land. Manuals introduced a degree of standardisation which greatly assists the modern researcher

---

85 Harvey, *Manorial Records*, esp. 6 and 19-20. For published texts see Oschinsky, *Walter of Henley* and Richardson and Sayles, *Fleta*.

when examining the records of courts held in different manors, but their authors were also keenly aware of the differences in local customs and usage. Many estate archives contain compilations of sections from the different manuals copied for ease of reference, perhaps by deputy stewards or young gentlemen as part of their training.

19 *(opposite page)* Bodrugan manor, Cornwall, 1696.
A small manor at which only eight jurors were sworn. Notable elements of this court baron include the appointment of a woman as reeve and the division of a whale seized by the steward and tenants.

The Homage afors[ai]d on thiere Corporall Oathes present all free and Convent[ia]ry ten[a]nts whoe owe any suite to this Court & have this day made defaulte.

They alsoe p[re]sent Eliz: Perking to doe the office of a Reeve for the ensueing for this Manno[u]r

They alsoe p[re]sent John Trestrayle to doe the office of a Tythingman for a tenem[en]t called Behago within the p[ar]ish of Cuby for the s[ai]d yeare

They alsoe p[re]sent that there was a greate Fish w[hi]ch some supposed to bee a very small whale, which came in betweene Nuge & the Deadman & siezed by the Stew[ar]d and severall of the tenau[n]ts to the Lord Use & Towed to Golona & Cut up & Boyled at Bodrugan, out of which came 3 hogsheads of Oyle, besides Abundanced carryed away by the Countrey.

Stewards and their deputies like Francis Rame, deputy steward of Havering in the later sixteenth century, might use their offices to their own profit and purchase property within the manor.[86] However, if they overstepped the mark, they could be called to account; complaints were made by tenants and a surveyor that the steward of Mere (Wiltshire), Sir Carew Raleigh, brother of Sir Walter Raleigh, had taken bribes to reduce entry fines and overlook sub-letting, and this led to his dismissal around 1623.[87]

20. Leven, Yorkshire, 1642.

Leaven Officers	Rob[er]te Bewell)	
	Henry Estrigge }	*Constables & sworne.*
Thomas Smyth	*William Walker}*	*bylawmen & sworne.*
Herbert Runton	*William Mawe)*	

Anthony Dandie   pinder [who kept the pound for stray animals] *sworne*
Thomas Wilson, Rob[er]te Ghossip   alefiners   sworne
Tho[mas] Smyth, Will[ia]m Mawe   Cargraves sworne.

---

86 McIntosh, *A community transformed*, 316.

87 Bettey, '"Ancient custom time out of mind", copyhold tenure in the west country' 314.

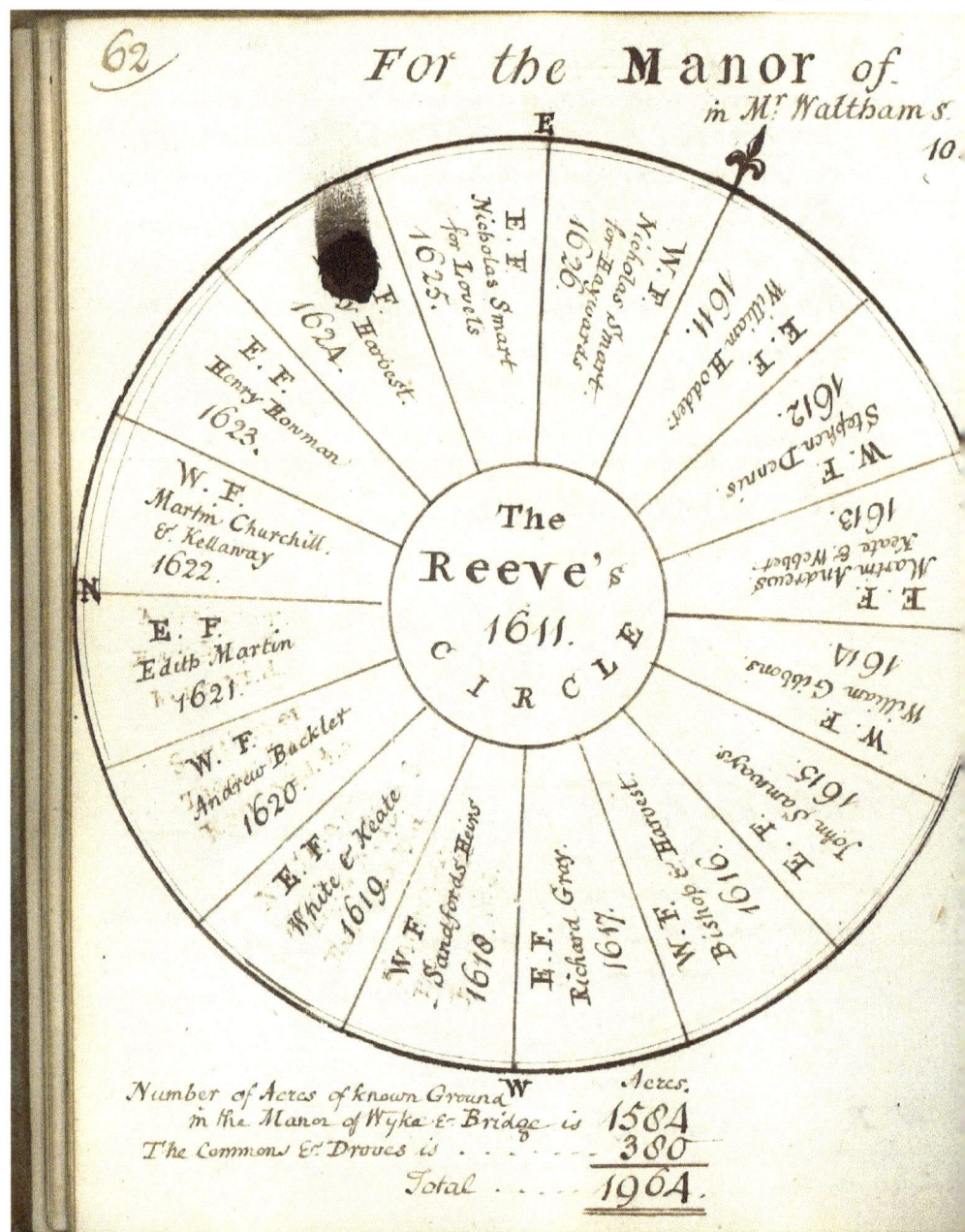

21. Wyke Regis Dorset, 1626.

Diagrams compiled by the steward of Wyke Regis, Dorset, in 1611 to show who would hold the offices of reeve and tithingman over the following years. Working clockwise around the reeve's circle, starting with William Hodder at 1 o'clock, each reeve is named for the next sixteen years.

MANORS AND MANORIAL DOCUMENTS AFTER 1500

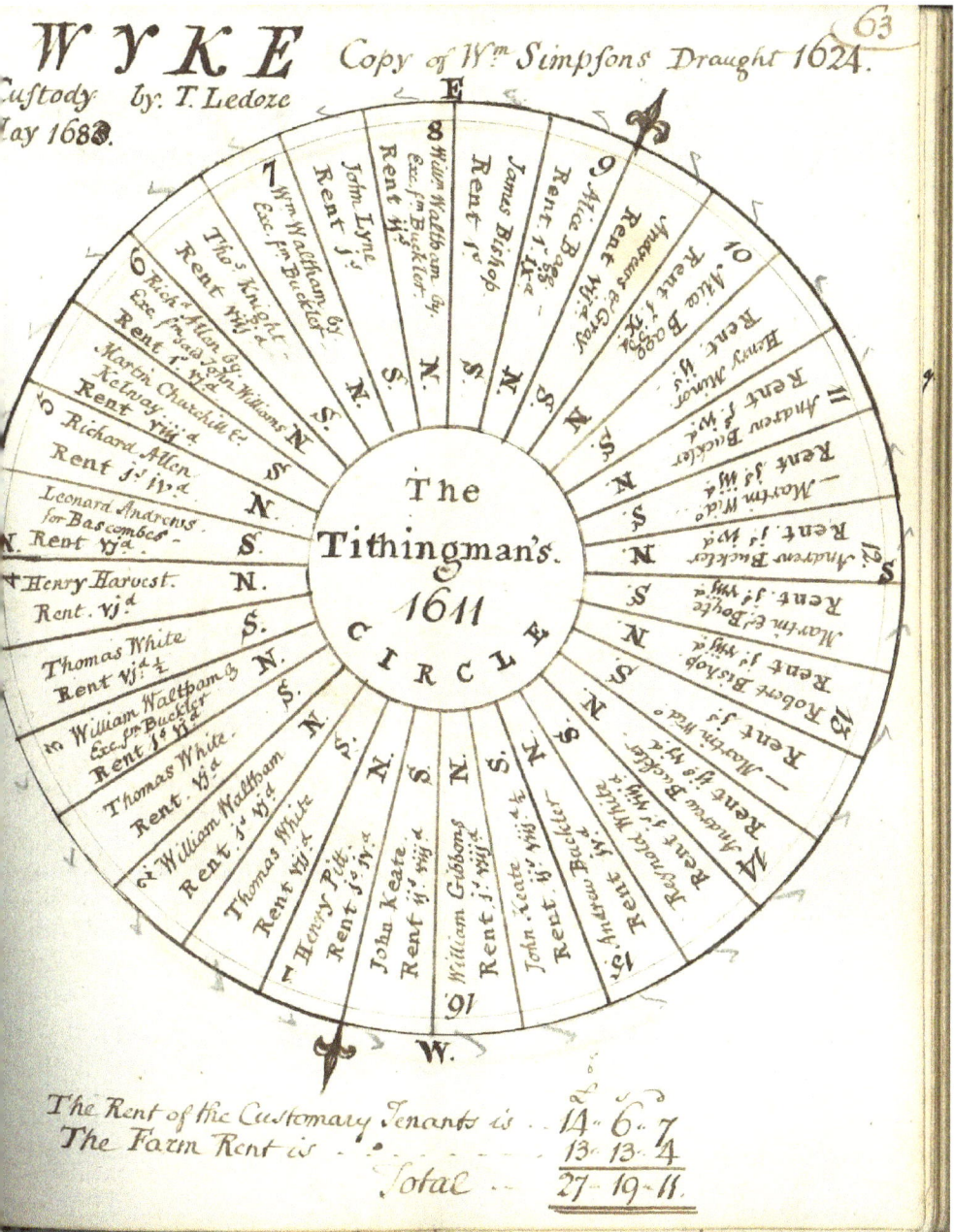

The tithingman's circle is more complicated than the reeve's. Wyke Regis was divided into two tithings: Northover and Southover (marked N and S in the circle). One tithingman was appointed to each tithing each year. Starting with Henry Pitt and Thomas White at 6 o'clock, and working clockwise to finish with John Keate and William Gibbons, each tithingman is named for the next sixteen years.

On larger manors, stewards were assisted by a deputy and everywhere there was a range of other officers whose names and duties varied between regions and manors. Typically, a rural manor might have a reeve, a hayward and two affeerers appointed at the Court Baron and a constable, tithingman and ale taster appointed at the Court Leet. On larger manors and in different areas, there might also be a beadle, pinders or pound keepers, deputy constables, shepherds and rent collectors, and in manors with an urban element there might be night watchmen, leather and meat inspectors and scavengers.

Farmers of demesnes were not officers of the court. Until the nineteenth century, the term 'farmer' had a technical and specific meaning, denoting someone who leased land for a fixed term in return for a cash payment. In a manorial context the term often applied specifically to the person who took the lease of all or part of the demesne. When holding a lease, the farmer retained some of the oversight of the manorial assets which had previously been the responsibility of the bailiff, particularly with reference to ensuring that mills, streams, barns, access routes and hedges were maintained. Where the demesne had been broken up and leased piecemeal, several farmers might have responsibility for different parts of the demesne and might in turn lease assets such as mills or warrens to a sub-tenant.

The reeve was the lord's principal officer appointed, often by rotation, at the Court Baron. He responsible for the day to day management of the manor in making sure that the other tenants fulfilled their customary obligations to the lord of the manor. Tenants served as reeves by election or in rotations of about every ten or fifteen years, depending on the size of the manor. It was a role that came with their tenement and in return they received a remission of all or part of their rent or an additional area of land linked to the office. Acting as reeve was probably not very popular and wealthier tenants, or widows who held tenements, often employed another tenant as a surrogate, since on most manors women were barred from holding offices. At Wakefield (Yorkshire) where the manor was divided into twelve 'graves', an officer known as a 'grave' or 'grieve' was selected by rotation, and often appointed a surrogate despite being assisted by a deputy or deputies.

Together with the reeve, the hayward, woodward and a harvest officer called a 'messor' were drawn from the tenants of the manor and their appontments registered at the Court Baron. They were responsible for maintenance of hay ricks, hedges, fences, common and open fields and management of coppice wood, and they set the dates at which certain resources could be exploited. Open fields, with general rotation, but in practice some choice and variety among the crops, had shared access routes to be acknowledged and maintained. Common meadows and pastures were divided according to a bewildering variety of local customs and numerous small regulatory decisions had to be made relating to trespass, fencing or encroachment throughout the year.

Most Courts Leet appointed constables who policed the community, arrested criminals and collected taxes. They were assisted by tithingmen, who were also drawn from among the tenants and often served by election or in rotation, and the assize of ale was overseen by ale-conners or ale tasters who ensured that beer was of merchantable quality and sold in standard measures. In addition to these three officers, who were common to most Courts Leet, additional officers were appointed depending upon local requirements. Where there was a tanning industry, scrutinisers were appointed to inspect the quality of the finished hides and disposal of waste products, night watchmen and light keepers might have a role in maintaining public order, particularly in manors with significant urban settlements. Ashton under Lyne (Lancashire) was heavily industrialised long before 1907, when the Webbs found that the court appointed a mayor, two high constables, four constables, twelve by-law men, an inspector of weights, a pounder, an ale taster and three bellmen.[88] In Lancashire, there were barleymen (from *byrlawman*) who administered bye-laws, hedgelookers and houselookers who ensured that hedges and houses were kept in good repair, and moss reeves who managed areas of turbary and regulated peat cutting. At the large manor of Havering (Essex), the lead officers were the homagemen, who were supported by bailiffs, constables, clerks of the market, sub-constables, woodwards, ale-tasters and marsh reeves.

Sometimes a hierarchy developed where younger men or the holders of smaller properties served in some offices, while others were reserved for older or wealthier tenants. Affeerers, sometimes called assessors, who set the levels of fines at the manor court, were selected as two of the older or wealthier tenants whose judgement might be respected by the rest of the homage. Some appointments were more arduous than others, some carried greater status and some had a ceremonial element. In most places, the manorial officers were part of a group who also served as parish and borough officers. At Earls Colne, the careers of manorial and parish officers in the early eighteenth century can be shown to be linked to the sizes of their tenements and also to the form of tenancy by which they held their land.[89] All tenants were subject to the judgements and decisions of the jurors and office holders of manorial court; many would serve as jurors and office holders at some time in their lives, so everyone could expect to regulate the activities of their neighbours and to be regulated by them.

9
The Customs of the Manor

Customs were derived from a series of precedents established by the lord, steward and tenants which regulated life on the manor in three main categories: customs of inheritance, customary obligations and customary rights. The customs were particular to each manor, sometimes differing between neighbouring manors in the same parish held by the same lord, and set limits upon the actions of both the lord and tenants. They appear in written form, called a custumal, from as early as the tenth century and survive in some numbers from the thirteenth century onwards.[90] Custumals, were often compiled as part of a survey which might identify those customs that were particular to a specific customary tenement, perhaps owing two days' work at harvest, and in a separate section identify those rights that were common to all tenants, that widows inherited without payment of a heriot or that all customary tenants might pasture their pigs in the woods between Michaelmas and Martinmas.

It was a primary function of the custumal to create good relations between lords and tenants to anticipate areas of conflict before they became disputes.[91] Administration and interpretation of customs was the responsibility of the jury

---

88 Webb and Webb, *English Local Government*, 115.

89 French and Hoyle, *The character of English rural society*, esp. 255-66.

90 Birrell, 'Manorial custumals reconsidered', 8-9.

91 Birrell, 'Manorial custumals reconsidered' 34-5.

at the manor court; they might seek recourse to custumals or court rolls to find evidence of the adoption or interpretation of a custom and higher courts were resistant to involvement in these disputes.[92] In theory, the customs of a manor had existed time out of mind and were unchanging, the written form of a custumal encouraged them to remain so from one generation to the next.[93] However, there are also examples of customs changing when it was mutually agreeable between the lord and tenants, or when a new set of circumstances presented a particular dilemma. The tenants of several manors belonging to Chertsey Abbey in Surrey changed their inheritance custom from ultimogeniture to primogeniture on payment of a collective fine to the Abbot, while at Gravely (Cambridgeshire) the change was made in the opposite direction.[94]

> 'Tis true, some of these Customs are very strange, such as that which was mentioned by the Lord Chief Justice Anderson, which he knew in the Manor of Wadhurst in Sussex, where he tells us, there are two Sorts of Copyhold Tenures, Sokeland and Bondland; and the Custom is, that if the Tenant was first admitted to Sokeland, and afterwards to Bondland, and died seised of both, his Heir at Law should inherit both; and if he was first admitted to Bondland, then his youngest Son should inherit both; but if he was admitted to both at the same Time, then his eldest Son should inherit both.

22. In one of many guides for manorial stewards and lawyers circulating in the eighteenth century William Nelson found it necessary to explain that some manorial customs were strange survivals in his own time and cites an example of one relating to an unusual instance of inheritance.

Customs of inheritance governed who had the right to be the next heir to a property and also the interest of widows. Usually, the eldest son was heir to a father's land, but occasionally inheritance by the youngest son (known as 'ultimogeniture'

---

92   Brooks, 'The agrarian problem in revolutionary England', 191-2.

93   Birrell, 'Manorial custumals reconsidered', 31-2 and 36-7.

94   Homans, *English Villagers*, 126.

or 'borough English') or partible inheritance (including 'gavelkind') was the custom. In the absence of sons, partible inheritance was most common among daughters with primogeniture an infrequent alternative. Widows usually had a right to hold their husband's estate for life, although on most manors this right was forfeited if they remarried or cohabited and the land passed to the next heir. Only customary land was subject to these inheritance restrictions and restricted by custom: freehold or leasehold could be gifted or left in a tenant's will to make provision for children who did not otherwise stand to inherit.

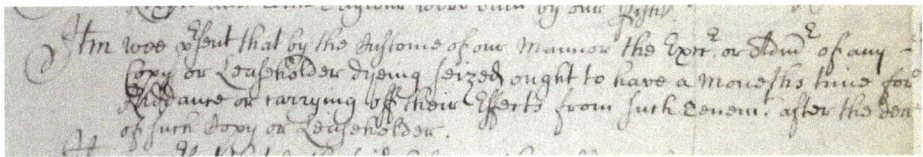

23. Horton, Dorset, 1650.
It[e]m wee p[re]sent that by the Custome of our Mannor the Exec[ut]our or Adm[inistrat]our of any Copy or Leaseholder dyeing seized ought to have a Moneths time for Riddance or carrying off their Effects from such tenem[en]t after the dea[th] of such Copy or Leaseholder.

Customs governing a tenant's obligations divided various tasks among those who held land. Many of these tasks originated from the tenants supplying some of the labour force for the land that was held in demesne by the lord; agricultural labour duties included ploughing, winnowing, carting, reaping and sowing. By the sixteenth century, only a few harvest time and carting services survived to supplement wage labour as most labour services had been commuted for monetary payments several generations, or even centuries, earlier. Where they survived they served as a marker for the former status of the land and represented a valuable addition to the lord's workforce at the busiest time of the year. In addition to providing a few days' labour the tenants were required, usually by election or rotation, to serve as officers such as reeves or haywards. The obligation to provide labour, usually converted to a cash rent, or serve as an officer was attached to the tenement. From the fifteenth century onwards where these holdings were broken up and sold by the acre, the obligation might then be attached to a small piece of land, so by the seventeenth century they often bore no relation to the size of a tenant's holding. A small piece of former villein land might have the services of reeve or tithingman attached to it as part of a rotation, when larger pieces of land did not.

Customary rights regulated the use of communal assets such as firewood, common grazing, areas of seasonal pasture, fishing and building materials, which allowed the tenants to supplement what they were able to produce from their tenement. Tenants might collect firewood in a specified location, pasture a certain number of animals on the commons according to the size of their tenement, or take timber allocated by the reeve to repair their buildings. The lord also had customary obligations to provide common assets, such as a boar, a ram or a mill, that would be used by the whole community, and also to maintain certain elements of common infrastructure like the pound for stray animals or the sheep dip. In Dorset, the responsibility to provide a bull fell to the farmer of the demesne at Piddlehinton in 1689; at Winterborne Monkton, it was, by custom, provided by the churchwardens out of the poor rate; while at Affpuddle, the manorial customs compiled in 1611 state that it was the parson who should provide both a bull and a boar.[95]

---

95 Bettey, '"Ancient custom time out of mind", copyhold tenure in the west country', 317.

The customs of a manor often appear archaic, so that when an eighteenth-century tenant is described as owing quit rents for his labour services, it appears that elements of medieval society persisted long into the modern world. Nevertheless, they represented distant memories and the actual labour services may not have been required for hundreds of years. The rights to common pasture or underwood for fuel were significant assets, and their removal would have caused genuine hardship. Despite this, the customs of the manor were more than a set of small rights and responsibilities; they were the defining set of common bonds which had been held by each community for hundreds of years, binding the lord to his tenants and providing a common sense of unity among the tenants of the difference between their manor and those of their neighbours. This social aspect of manorial life is highlighted at Brinkworth (Wiltshire) in 1645 when the jurors at the Court Leet complained that the lord's farmer had, contrary to their custom, failed to provide a dinner for the jury.[96]

In the south-west in the sixteenth and seventeenth centuries, the customs associated with copyholds governed all aspects of farming practice, transfer of holdings, entry fines, rents, heriots, rules of cultivation, access to common grazing, wood, stone, fuel and the rights of widows.[97] At Norton Bavant (Wiltshire) in the early seventeenth century, a dispute over tenants' rights of fishing in the river was settled by an appeal to the oldest inhabitants, who swore it was an ancient custom. At Mere (Wiltshire) in 1603, the courts of the adjacent manors of Woodlands and Zeals Clevedon had been held together for a century when a dispute arose over inheritance and it was necessary to establish whether only the widow of the first-named copyholder had the right to inherit her husband's tenement. The steward searched the individual court rolls for both manors back to 1380, the results showing that the custom was different on these two manors, and by doing so he created a useful summary of the earlier cases from rolls that have not survived.

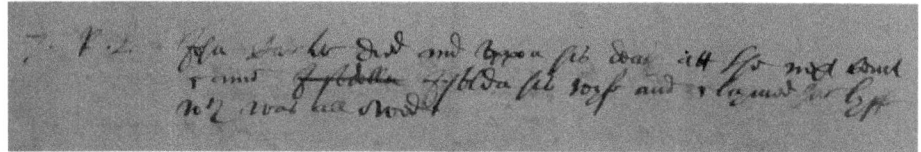

24. Zeals Clevedon manor, 1603.
7 R 2 [the seventh year of the reign of Richard II, 1383-1384] *John Carter died and uppon his death att the next court came ~~Isabella~~ Isolda his wyfe and claymed her lyff w[hi]^{ch} was allowed.*

On most manors, the customs are only known because they were mentioned individually in presentments or court rolls. A *Custumal*, a formal record of the customs of a manor, was not often produced and these documents do not survive in large numbers. They may be found within court books and bundles of stewards' papers, many were cited in legal disputes and consequently many survive, and have been indexed, in the Exchequer class E134 at The National Archives. The customs of a manor, when written down, were by their nature archaic recordings of historic rights and obligations drawn from the collective memory of the homage and steward. For this reason, they were valued and used in arbitration. Many written sets of customs were explicitly drawn up following consultation with the eldest

---

96   Crowley, *Court records of Brinkworth and Charlton*, 232.

97   Bettey, '"Ancient custom time out of mind", copyhold tenure in the west country, 307-22.

inhabitants of the manor and include rights that were known to exist although they may have become obsolete many years earlier. It seems very unlikely that in the eighteenth century, the lord of the manor of Puddletown (Dorset) was able to enforce a custom that only allowed litigation between tenants to take place in his own court and barred them from taking cases to Chancery, but this custom is still recorded. On other manors, the custom that all tenants must grind their corn in the lord's mill is recorded in the eighteenth and nineteenth centuries when it had ceased to be enforced. Sometimes the lord's mill no longer existed and all the arable had been converted to pasture, but the custom remained. The rights and responsibilities that were current at any particular moment can be identified with greater certainty as they were tested by the lord and the tenants in the records of the manorial court.

The following example from Okeford Fitzpaine (Dorset) reveals the broad range of aspects of life on the manor that might be covered by the customs. Many of the customs relate to the rights and procedures governing copyhold land, such as who had the right to inherit and what fines they should pay. Others concern procedural rules such as the appointment of attorneys or where out of court surrenders and admissions could be made. Some customs, like those regarding grinding corn and trespass litigation, are restrictive to the tenants and protect the rights of the lord securing the mill's profits and the fines paid in his courts. Others benefited the tenants by giving them rights to firewood, chalk and the appointment of assessors of fines. Those customs regarding timber for repairs were of mutual benefit as it was in the interests of both lord and tenant that the copyholds were well maintained.

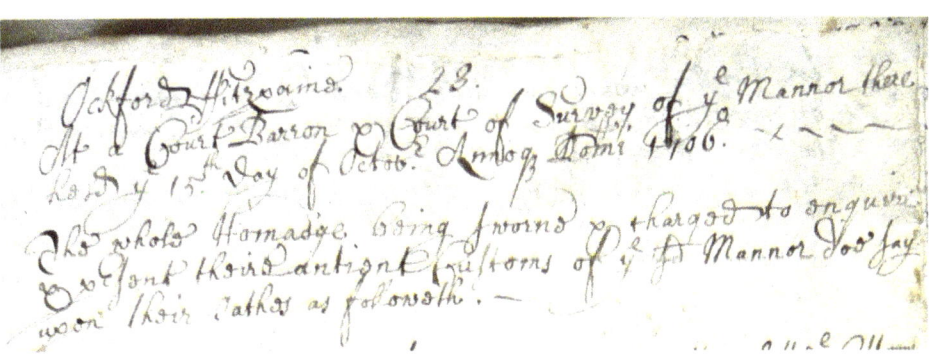

25. *Ockford Fitzpaine: At a Court Barron & Court of Survey of the Mannor there held the* 15*th day of October Annoq[ue] Dom[in]i* 1706
The whole Homadge being sworne & charged to enquire & p[re]sent theire ancient Customs of the s[ai]d Mannor doe say upon their Oathes as followeth:

> The lord of the manor may grant customary tenements for one, two or three lives.
> The lord and his officers may make contracts to grant land out of the court, but within the manor.
> No tenant may sue another tenant for trespass in any court other than the manor court.
> All tenants must pay their rents at the four usual quarter days.
> All widows are entitled to hold their husband's lands unless they remarry, but the estate is subject to a heriot on their death or surrender of the property.
> Tenants may fell any dead trees except timber trees: elm, ash and oak.
> No tenant may lease all or part of his land for more than one year without a licence from the lord of the manor.
> Any tenant may pass his copyhold to one of the other lives on the copyhold agreement without paying a fine.
> Any tenant who sells his land without licence forfeits his claim to it, but any other lives

on the copyhold are unaffected and may still hold the land.

The lord is responsible for providing timber for all repairs [to buildings]. The timber may be from the tenant's own lands or requisitioned from other customary tenements.

Each tenant is allowed the branches and tops of timber trees felled on their tenement, and for each tree felled the recipient of the timber is to plant four replacements.

All tenants may take fuel from the common and lanes.

A tenant may surrender his land out of court in the presence of two or three other tenants.

Tenants are entitled to chalk from the pit on Common Downe to repair their tenements.

Tenants may lop and top those trees on their tenements.

No tenant may let or lease his lands to a stranger if there is an existing tenant who will pay the same rent.

All tenants must grind corn at the customary mill and bake at the customary oven.

All tenants should attend the manor court if given warning that it is to be held.

All amercements are to be assessed by two assessors from among the homage.

All tenants are to keep their houses, hedges, ditches and fences well repaired.

The fine of £5 is set for any tenant who removes impounded cattle from the lord's pound.

A heriot is due on the death, forfeiture or surrender of any tenant, payable from their estate. The heriot is to be the best beast selected by the bailiff and three or four tenants.

If a copyhold is granted for two lives, and the first tenant dies before taking possession, then the second tenant shall take it without an entry fine.

Tenants are to maintain all of the lord's houses on their tenements with his timber, and to maintain their own buildings with their own timber.

All tenants are to have *plough boott* and *fire boott* [timber to maintain ploughs and fire wood] supplied by the lord's officers.

Any tenant may surrender his tenement through an appointed attorney.

Any incoming tenant has the first option to purchase the animal given as heriot from the previous tenant's estate before it is offered to anyone else.

All orders and presentments made by the tenants at the lord's court are to be observed by all tenants unless the majority disagree with the order and have the consent of the steward in not complying.

Tenants may store their brushwood or underwood in their hedges.

If a tenant dies then his executor is to manage his estate until the next quarter day.

Tenants pasturing sheep on the common down are to pay 12d. per sheep: 6d. to the lord and 6d. to the shepherds.

The tenants pay the rector 3d. per acre for meadow, 3d. for each cow and 2d. for each heifer in lieu of tithes and all other things in kind.

Signed: Richard Williams and Henry Hony, with the marks of Simon Hardy, John Harber, Christopher Rose and John Drake.

At Okeford Fitzpaine, the core customs are medieval in origin, namely the rights to fuel and timber for repairs, the rights to common pasture, the obligations to use the lord's mill and oven. Others clearly do not originate from beyond the 'memory of man' (legally before 1189), such as the high levels of the fines, appointment of attorneys, and restrictions on the courts that could be used to prosecute trespass; these all date from the sixteenth century or later. Customs could be adapted, or inserted, by the consent of the steward and homage. Others remained as archaic survivals and were regarded as quaint or perplexing by later antiquarians. The Rev. Collinson, writing his *History of Somerset* in the late eighteenth century, remarked on the curious custom that at the manor of Taunton for the youngest son to inherit copyhold land rather than the eldest.[98] This practice was a form of inheritance known as ultimogeniture or 'borough English'. At Kilmersdon, he observed that if

---

98   Collinson, *History of Somerset*, vol. 3, 233.

a widow was not chaste, she forfeited the customary lands held from her deceased husband unless she entered the following court riding on a ram and made an open acknowledgement to the steward.[99] Public humiliation was not the mainstay of manorial customs; they were often designed to bind the community together. At West Hatch on Christmas day, the lord provided every householder with a loaf of bread and a pound and a half of beef and pork as well as their evening meal.[100]

26. Rewe manor, Devon.
Item *by o[ur] custome the Reve of the Mannor is to gather the Lord[es] rente of all the customary and convencionary ten[au]nt[es] quarterly and all other dutyes and at thende* [the end] *of the yeare to pay the same to the lord[es] and is to have five shilling[es] for his fee beinge always heretofore allowed him by the Lorde at the tyme of the passing[es] of his accompte* [account]

10
Land Management Records Produced Outside the Court

Manorial records such as court books, court rolls, presentments and copyhold agreements were produced at, or resulted directly from, the court in session. Other records, such as accounts, rent rolls, rentals and maps were the products of the steward's management of the manor outside the court. A further group of documents, including surveys, extents, perambulations and custumals might be informed by a special session of the Court Baron or produced independently.

Accounts for the whole manor were long and detailed documents in the thirteenth and fourteenth centuries. Before the demesne was leased, accounts listed the lord's income through rents, profits of the courts, livestock, harvested grains, wool, hides, cheeses and other produce and the expenses or discharges during the course of the year. Such detailed accounts survive only occasionally from the sixteenth century; once the demesne had been leased there was no longer a range of items to be valued and accounts became much simpler documents. Where detailed accounts were maintained, they were compiled using a format

---

99   Collinson, *History of Somerset*, vol. 2, 446.

100 Collinson, *History of Somerset*, vol. 2, 180.

27. *(opposite)* Chippenham, Sheldon and Lowdon manor, Wiltshire, 1730

The Mannor of Chippenham Sheldon and Lowdon		23th Aprill 1730		

Rents Rec[eiv]ed by Sam[uel] Martyn for the Use of
John Norris Esq[uire] and due at Lady day [25 March] last

	£	s	d
of the Widow Mary Brooks for 7 } years quit rent due for the House in } poss[essi]on of Jos[eph] Russ }		14	
of Joseph Archard 5 years & halfe	5	10	
of Richard White 5 years and an } halfe }		5	6
of James Alden for the like	1	7	6
of Mrs Bushell for the like		13	9
of William Tranter for late Heads } for the like time }		13	9
of John Harris for the like		13	9
of William Aust for the like		5	6
of John Simpkins for \late/ Salters four } years and an halfe }		4	6
of Moses Pollard for 5 years & ½		5	6
of Richard Russ Es[qui]r[e] of Rob[er]t } Coles 4 y[ea]rs & ½ at lady day 1729 } for Williams's and Coles Tenem[en]t }			9
[Continues]			

Note: the entries for William Tranter and John Simpkins provide the surnames of former tenants, Head and Salter.

---

that conformed to the standard medieval pattern: all the profits were listed under their respective headings, providing a total of the income received, followed by all expenses, a total of disbursements and interim payments, and a final total.

When the demesne was retained in hand or leased to a farmer, accounts usually simply showed the total rents, profits of the courts and perhaps income from a residual dovecot, fishpond or corn mill. A lessee was not a manorial officer and unless he adopted the role of the bailiff or reeve, it was necessary to appoint a rent collector who sometimes submitted a separate account. Thus the standardisation of the medieval accounts was gradually abandoned and the use of English text and Arabic numerals became more common. More detailed accounts were kept for assets which fell under the direct management of the steward or the manorial officers, either as an individual account when the timber from a wood was harvested or the cargo from a wreck was salvaged, or as an annual account for a market, shooting or fishing. For instance, at Crediton (Devon), the steward of the manor kept a separate series of market accounts for much of the nineteenth century. Rights to extract minerals below the soil had always been a source of profit and lords often retained chalk and lime quarries in hand. As demand for coal increased, some lords found that they possessed a more significant resource; at Madeley (Shropshire), the manor administered the mines' duty return as late as 1910.

The profits of the manorial court, known as perquisites, payments made on every manor in all periods, were sometimes extracted into separate lists for ease of accounting. Some fines, such as those for non-attendance, were set at customary rates and yielded little income. Those that could be varied, such as trespass with livestock or assault. In theory, fines for any individual offence brought before a

> The Mannor of Chippenham
> Sheldon and Lowdon — 23th Aprill 1730
>
> Rents Rec'd by Sam:ll Martyn for the use of
> John Norris Esq:r and due at Lady day last
>
> | | £ | s | d |
> |---|---|---|---|
> | Of the Widow Mary Brooks for 7 years quit rent due for ye Houseing possess'n of Jos: Russ | | 14 | .. |
> | of Joseph Orchard 5 years c halfe | | 10 | — |
> | of Richard White 5 years and an halfe | | 5 | 6 |
> | of James Oldenfor ye like | | 7 | 6 |
> | of Mrs Bushell for ye like | | 13 | 9 |
> | of William Trainton for Cato Heads for the like time | | 13 | 9 |
> | of John Harris for the like | | 13 | 9 |
> | of William Aust for the like | | 5 | 6 |
> | of John Shepheard for ye late Sallers foure years and an halfe | | 4 | 6 |
> | of Moses Pollard for 5 years c ½ | | 5 | 6 |
> | of Richard Russ Ex:r of Robt. Coles 4 y:rs c ½ at Lady day 1729 for Williams's and Coles Tenem:t | | 9 | — |
> | Of Trisham Gibbs and Robert |

manorial court were limited to a maximum of 40s., but as we have seen at Okeford Fitzpaine, a fine of £5 was set in the customs for the removal of animals from the lord's pound.

Rent rolls may also be considered to be a form of account when they provide the sums that were to be paid by each tenant or an indication that rents had been paid in a given term or year. Most rent rolls only contain the name of the current tenant and the amount to be paid. Otherwise, they sometimes show the amount payable at the four quarter days when the rent was due, at or around the feasts of Michaelmas (29 September); Christmas (25 December); Lady Day (25 March), and St John the Baptist (24 June). When the rent had been paid, the steward often annotated the roll next to the tenant's name and occasionally the same roll was

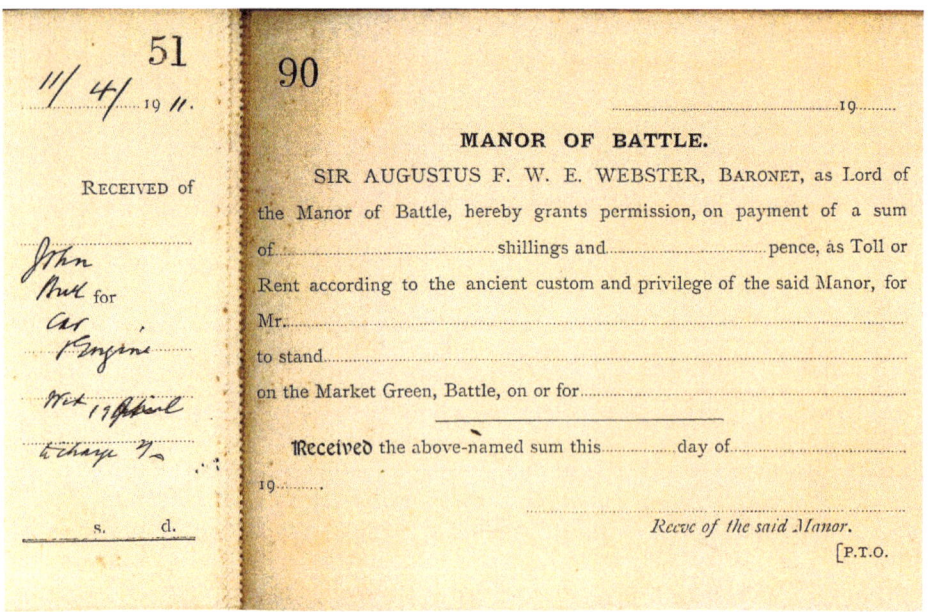

28. Battle manor, East Sussex 1911.
A printed receipt book for payments to the lord of the manor for stalls at Battle market.

used for several years with a separate column for payments in each year. Some rent rolls were compiled for particular forms of rent, such as quit rents for commuted services, or rents due at certain times of the year.

Surveys were written accounts of the manor providing a description of its boundaries, fields, woods, commons and all other assets as well as a detailed rental. Some surveys were made with the agreement of the tenants, as mentioned above, often following a special court of survey held by the steward, and sometimes a professional surveyor was employed to take accurate measurements. A survey might contain the name of each tenant, other names on copyholds and their ages, any agricultural services owed by the tenement holder, the heriot, entry fine and annual rent, and a comprehensive list of all land held by that tenant from the lord of the manor, often with field names and acreages. Although some are simply surveys of the lands leased to tenants, in effect a very detailed rental, most also include details of the land held directly by the lord, or leased to a farmer, such as the demesne farm, woods, mills, quarries and rabbit warrens as well as common land and open sheep pasture. Besides listing all the land under the heading of each tenant, it was also common to produce a summary listing of the acreage of each type of land: arable, pasture, meadow, woodland and common, sometimes divided into individual fields or areas. Surveys provided the steward with the details of the lands, infrastructure and tenancies that he needed to manage the manor. They were comprehensive and expensive to produce and consequently produced infrequently. As noted above, they were often compiled as the result of a change of ownership and in place of a court of recognition, so the new lord had a comprehensive assessment of his new property, or when a major structural change had taken place such as the enclosure of common fields. Many former monastic manors had new surveys made by their new owners in the later sixteenth century and The National Archives holds large numbers of Commonwealth surveys drawn up for those lands that were administered by Parliamentary officers, 1650-1659.

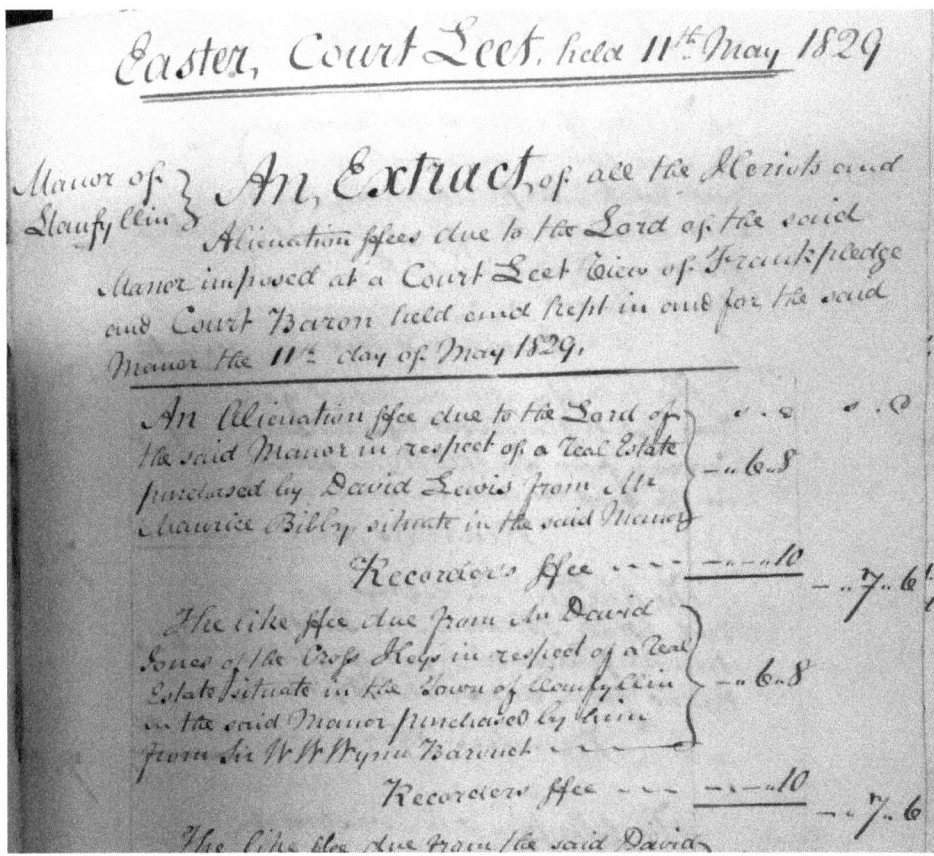

29. Account book, Llanfyllin, Powys, 1829.

Manor of Llanfyllin: An Extract of all the Heriots and Alienation Fees due to the Lord of the said Manor imposed at a Court Leet View of Frankpledge and Court Baron held and kept in and for the said Manor the 11th day of May 1829.
An Alienation Fee due to the Lord of the said Manor in respect of a Real Estate purchased by David Lewis from Mr Maurice Bibby, situate in the said Manor 6s 8d
Recorders Fee, 10d
[Total] 7s 6d
The like fee due from Mr David Jones of the Cross Keys in respect of a Real Estate situate in the Town of Llanfyllin in the said Manor purchased by him from Sir W W [Watkin Williams] Wynn Baronet 6s 8d
Recorders Fee, 10d
[Total] 7s 6d.

Surveys can provide considerable evidence of landscape features and the arrangement of agricultural land even when they are not accompanied by a map. earlier surveys tended to concentrate upon the status of the land: demesne, freehold or customary, whereas later surveys were more concerned with land use: arable, pasture, woods and meadow. the information recorded might vary considerably and depended upon the reasons why the steward had thought it necessary to compile a survey at that time. The following example was produced in 1584 for Okeford Fitzpaine (Dorset), where the common fields had recently been enclosed and it was convenient for the surveyor to arrange his survey with all of a single tenant's holdings listed under their name:[101]

> Edward Howe holds by copy one tenement with garden and croft adjacent between the tenement of Henry Reynolde on the south, the tenement of Agnes Mahoe on the north and abutting to the east over the Queen's highway leading from Sturmestur to Blandford, containing 2 roods 5 perches.
> He also holds similarly by the west boundary of the aforesaid croft one inclosure called Westwood lying in two sections between the customary land of Henry Wakeford, Joseph Harrys and William Chipman to the south, the land of diverse tenements to the north, abutting to the east over the aforesaid croft and the croft of Henry Reynold and to the west over the lands of diverse men, containing 6 acres, 1 rood, 30 perches.
> He also holds similarly one inclosure called the Castle lying between the land of William White senior to the west, the land of Elizabeth Saye to the east, abutting to the north over the land of the aforesaid Elizabeth and to the south over the land of William White senior and Edward How, containing 7 acres, 3 roods, 20 perches.
> He also holds similarly two inclosures lying together called Emede between the land of William White senior, Agnes Mahoe and Agnes Whyte to the west, the land of John Shotto to the east, abutting over the aforesaid close called Castle to the north and over the land of Edward How and Agnes White, widow, to the south, containing altogether 6 acres, 3 roods.
> He also holds similarly one inclosure called Longclosse lying between the aforesaid Emede to the north, the meadow of William Ford to the south, abutting to the east over the meadow of Agnes White called Millclosse and to the southwest over a certain lane leading to the mill called Emede Lane, containing 1 acre, 2 roods, 13 perches.
> He also holds one inclosure called Narbor lying in two squares between the land of Richard Gobye and William Forde to the south, the tenement of William Chipman and Agnes White to the north, abutting to the west over Narbor Lane and to the east over a certain lane leading to the Downes called Knill Lane, containing 10 acres, 1 rood.
> He also holds several closes lying together called Southleys lying in diverse sections between the land of George Trencher esquire in the parish of Bell [Belchalwell] to the west, the land of Thomas White esquire lying in the parish of Eberton [Ibberton] and the land of diverse tenements called Whitmere to the east, abutting to the north over the land of John Iles and Elizabeth Saye and over the common river bank to the south west, containing altogether 56 acres, 2 roods, 32 perches.
> He also holds one inclosure near Horsfoole Plecke lying between the land of Agnes White to the north, the land of Edward Williams to the south, abutting to the east over the common river bank and to the west over Mill Lane, containing 2 acres 2 roods.
> [Marginal annotation: total acreage:] 92 acres 2 roods, 6 perches

When land was held in an open field and several tenants held successive strips it might be more convenient to list each strip in turn. In the following example from Durweston (Dorset) a group of strips was listed sequentially in a *precinct* or *stadium*, which was probably recognisable as an area defined by roads or hedges:[102]

---

101 Palmer, *Three Tudor Surveys*, 71-2.

102 Palmer, *Three Tudor Surveys*, 170.

> Stadium abutting towards the east over the aforesaid stadium going towards the ~~south~~ north.
> John Howe holds one inclosure lying between the aforesaid way to the south and South Cliffe to the north abutting towards the east over the aforesaid close and containing 4 acres.
> And there is next vacant land called The South Cliffe.
> John Henning holds near there 1 acre.
> The same holds near the same 1 acre.
> John Iles holds 1 acre.
> Hugh Dashwood holds 1 acre.
> John Vallevine holds 3 acres.
> And there is one piece of land containing half an acre called The Tything Man's Place which is allowed every year to him that is the tithingman.
> John Stevens holds 1 acre.
> John Sheperd holds 1 acre
> John Rogers holds 2 acres.
> Alice Dennis holds 2 acres.
> John Rogers holds 1 acre.
> Edith Rogers holds 1 acre.
> Richard Prower holds 2 acres.

These two Dorset surveys were produced for the same lord within a year of each other for manors barely ten miles apart, yet their format is quite different as the surveyors represented the physical layout of the fields. But neither survey provides much evidence of how the land was held. Elsewhere, surveyors, perhaps charged with a different remit, included more information relating to how the land was held. At Walsham-le-Willows (Suffolk), an extraordinary survey produced in 1577 provides information relating to topography, tenures and the division of the land between several manors:[103]

> Robwood John senior, the said customary close sometymes Packes nowe in the tenure of the said John Robwoodwith a parcell of the foresaid lane lyinge into it conteyninge x perches is holden of the manor of Walsham Churchowse by coppy ot courte roll and lyeth northe by his laste said customary close sowthe by a customary close of pasture growndein the tenure of Steven Hawes called Penns Meare este uppon Ronnelles Lane and weste uppon the foresaid crofte of John [Robwood] and conteyneth – ij acres xxxv perches.
> Hawes Stephen. The said customary close of pasture grownde called Penns Meare sometymesas it semeth iiij^{or} or v percelles and nowe lynge all into one in tenure of Steven Hawes (who claymethe he hath one acre of free grownde within the same) holden of [blank] lyeth toward the este betwene Cowe Lyser aforesaid and toward the west betwene a customary close of pasture grownde called Sopers Crofte in the tenure of the said Steven, and in part a customary croft holden of the manor of Church Howse the northe hed wherof butteth upon a lane there called Ronnelles Lane, and the sowth hed butteth uppon Upp Strete and conteyneth – viij acres di. [*dimidium, half*] j rod xvij perches.

Another important aspect of some surveys was to record the rents, fines and heriots payable by the tenants as well as the terms of copyholds. Recording this information was not the principal function of surveys and it was often confined to

---

103 Dodd, *The field book of Walsham-le-Willows*, 114.

the more frequently produced rentals, as the details of heirs and entry fines would quickly become outdated. The following example from the manor of Langton Wallis (Dorset) is from a particularly detailed survey drawn up in 1585, which was intended to provide a complete view of a set of manors that had recently been acquired by the Tudor courtier Sir Christopher Hatton:[104]

> Walter Thomse holds to him, to John his son, and Richard Thomse the son of Robert Thomse for term of their lives successively by a copy sealed and subscribed by the said William Grove, steward, dated 23rd September year 16th Queen Elizabeth [1574] which contains:
>
> | | |
> |---|---|
> | Item, the house with the ground adjoining to the same | 3 a., 0 r., 0 p. |
> | Item, 2 closes of pasture called Heath Feelde | 9 a., 2 r., 38 p. |
> | Item, 1 close of pasture called Norlege | 7 a., 1 r., 38 p. |
> | Item, 2 closes of arable against his house | 11 a., 3 r., 29 p. |
> | Item, 1 close next the sea side | 14 a., 0 r., 28 p. |
> | [Total] | 46 a., 1 r., 13 p. |
>
> The same Walter Thomse pays for his yearly rent 13s. 6d. and for a parcel of the demesnes held at will 2d. and for customary works 4d. The fine paid at the taking of his farm £50. Heriot 1.
>
> Richard Trewe holds to him, to Mary and Rebecca for term of their lives successively by a copy of the demise of Sir Francis Williughbye, knight, and subscribed by William Grove, steward, dated 23rd September year 17th Queen Elizabeth [1575] which contains one tenement, viz.:
>
> | | |
> |---|---|
> | Item, the tenement with a parcel of meadow | 1 a., 3 r., 17 p. |
> | Item, a close of pasture called Wood Close | 2 a., 3 r., 9 p. |
> | Item, 2 closes of pasture shonting on Langton Matrevers common | 8 a., 1 r., 24 p. |
> | Item, a close against the house, arable | 10 a., 0 r., 0 p. |
> | Item, a close of arable among the grounds by the sea side | 11 a., 2 r., 9 p. |
> | Item, 2 closes of meadow adjoining to Langton Matreveres common | 3 a., 0 r., 1 p. |
> | Item, one other great close of pasture | 11 a., 2 r., 22 p. |
> | [Total] | 49 a., 1 r., 3 p. |
>
> The same Richard Trewe pays for his yearly rent 15s. 8d. and for a parcel of the demesne held at will for 2d. and for customary works 4d. The fine paid at the taking of his farm 40s. Heriot 1.

In the above example the entry fine of £50 paid by Walter Thomse indicates how far the value of customary tenements increased after the annual rents had become fixed. The lord of the manor was unable to raise the rent or the payment for customary works that had been commuted, often centuries previously. Nevertheless, the amount of the entry fine was entirely at his discretion and in this case the last time it had been paid it was almost 75 times the annual rent.

A survey might be made of part of the manor. Surveys of arable land, downs, meadows or pastures were made in response to disputes, enclosure or rearrangement of tenancies. The demesnes were often surveyed at the beginning and end of a lease and those assets kept in hand by the lord, such as quarries, woods or the timber trees on the tenant's holdings, were surveyed so the steward and manorial officers knew their long term value.

Rentals usually contain the names of current freehold and copyhold tenants as well as the names, number and ages of the additional lives on the copyhold tenancies

---

104 Forrest, Halling Barnard, Mitchell and Papworth, *Ralph Treswell's survey*, 166.

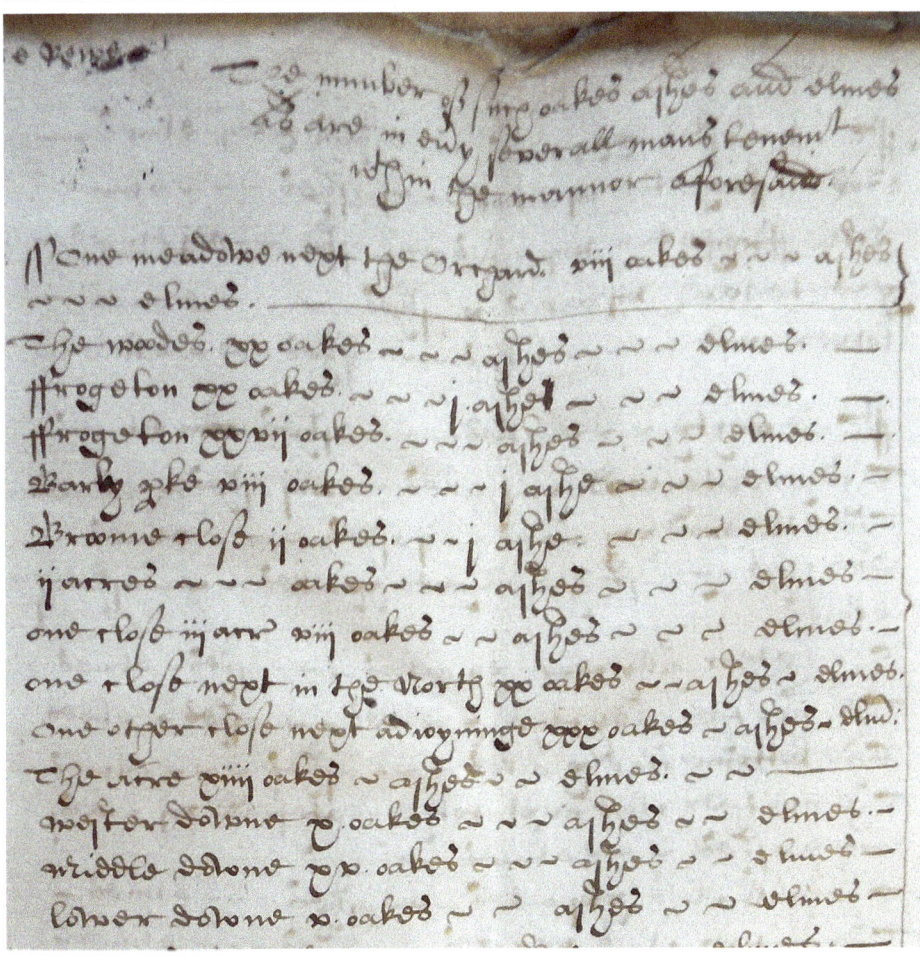

30. Rewe manor, Devon, 1619.
The start of a survey of trees on each of the tenements on the manor which remained the property of the lord.

Rewe   The number of such oakes and elmes
as are in ev[er]y severall mans tenem[en]t
w[i]thin the mannor aforesaid

One meadowe next the Orchard, viij oakes – – – ashes - - - elmes
The woodes, xx oakes - - - ashes - - - elmes
Frogeton, xx oakes - - - i ashes - - - elmes
Frogeton, xxvij oakes - - - ashes - - - elmes
Barly p[ar]ke, viij oakes - - - i ashes - - - elmes
Broome close, ij oakes - - - i ashes - - - elmes
ij acres, - - - oakes - - - ashes - - - elmes
one close iij acres, viij oakes - - - ashes - - - elmes
one close next in the north, xx oakes - - - ashes - - - elmes
one other close next adjoyninge, xxx oakes - - - ashes - - - elm[es]
The Acre, viij oakes - - - ashes - - - elmes
Wester Downe, x oakes - - - ashes - - - elmes
Middle Downe, xv oakes - - - ashes - - - elmes
Lower Downe, v oakes - - - ashes - - - elmes

and the amount of rent owed each year. Sometimes they also include brief details of the tenements, but this information is not as comprehensive as what would be found in a survey. They generally also include notes about entry fines and heriots, when they were payable and what was paid at the last admission. Rentals were drawn up more frequently than surveys; the information they contain had some longevity beyond the date of compilation, and they are frequently annotated with changes of tenants or notes about the ages of the remaining lives attached to copyholds and leases. Eventually they became obsolete and a new rental was compiled, but the old one was often kept as a point of reference. Thus a collection of rentals is invaluable in providing snapshots of the whole manor at a series of fixed points.

Rentals and surveys can be used in combination to track property holdings and changes in land use over a long period. At Chippenham (Cambridgeshire), a survey of 1544 was already partially obsolete by the time a full rental was produced in 1560. In 1636, both documents were annotated with the names of later tenants, and in 1712, a comprehensive survey and estate map gave details of the acreage of every strip in the open fields and described the village so accurately that the 1544 survey can be plotted onto it.[105]

31. Rental, Ilmington, Warwickshire, 1627.

The Mannor of Ilmington in the Countye of warwicke whereof the gretest p[ar]te Lyeth in the Comon feldes Nycholas Sowthorne and Will[ia]m Rose for the farme   *p[er] ann[um]*
house 3 Litle Closes adjoininge w[i]th 2 ground[es] called
swacom[e] & waleworthe w[hi]ch be well wooded & to be cut   036 00 00
for the Lo[rd] every 22th yeare and a close of Meadow
w[hi]ch was p[ar]cell of the wood Contening together
of them for 3 yard Land on the west hill w[i]th theire   030 00 00
appurtenac[es]

Estate and manorial maps began to be produced during the reign of Elizabeth I, but they were expensive to produce and very rare before the eighteenth century. Although some maps were schematic, even from the late sixteenth century manorial maps could be very accurate and might be used in legal disputes. Map-making relied upon skilled professional surveyors and cartographers being employed by the lord and his steward often when there was

---

105 Spufford, *Contrasting communities*, 58-92.

a boundary dispute or sale of the manor. Maps were sometimes annotated when fields were divided, commons enclosed or farms sold. They provide a reminder that land use was never static, constantly changing and developing to take account of changes in the rural economy, while the boundaries of the manors remained unaltered over centuries.

The information contained within a map can shed light on previous land use. Field names may indicate the former use of a field for a different form of agriculture or the presence of a demolished building. Some cartographers were very precise, so depictions of 'S' shaped strips in fields may indicate medieval ploughing with oxen, while those with straight sides would be more likely to be found in more recently enclosed land.[106]

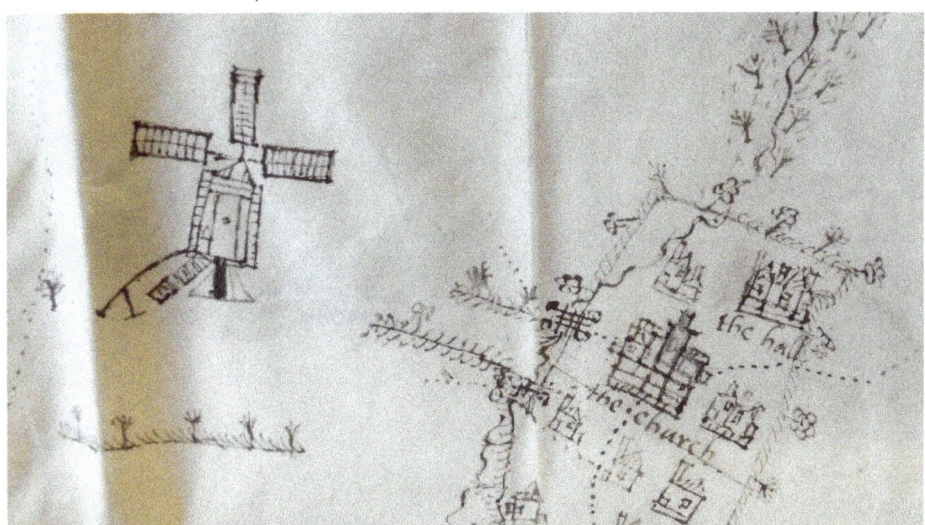

32 and 33. Two maps of Beeby, Leicestershire.
In 1617 the manor contained several large open fields and supported a windmill and manor house called 'the hall'. In 1672 the fields had been enclosed for pasture, the windmill and hall had disappeared, but were still remembered in the field names 'mill closes' and 'North Hall close'.

---

106 Eyre, 'The curving plough strip and its historical implications', 80-94.

34. Pennance manor, in St Budock Parish, Cornwall, 1769.

The surveyor, Simon Dell of Falmouth, has divided the manor into six sections. Each section has a a reference table containing the names of the closes or fields and the acres, rods and perches according to scales of both statutary and customary acres. Some areas have

names revealing their use: 'Mowhay', 'Milking Yard', 'Little Common', 'Calves Meadow', 'The Orchard' and the quarries at 'Whim Pitt'. Springs, wells, roads, cliffs and the high and low water marks on the beaches; some of the footpaths now form part of the Southwest Coastal Path.

35. Feckenham manor, Worcestershire, 1591.
This perambulation of the ancient demesne boundaries of Feckenham manor, Worcestershire, based upon the oral testimony of old men, includes field names, landmarks, routes of paths and footpaths and the names of tenants.
The true Compasse of Auncient Demeanes by the Report of old men.
Imprimis [Firstly] *begininge at Nowers greene soe alonge Backsters Lane by the nether end of wood Perrisill to the Berrowe gate then goeinge by the Rouwe of houses called the Berrowe leavinge out the Assarts leadinge unto a Lane called the Berrowe lane soe up the Banner way* neare *unto Bishopps fields soe goeinge the Banner waye neare unto the wall house all one the right hand is Auncyent Demeasnes and still continuing in the Banner way untill you come unto Mente Fieldes nere unto Gould Fields soe keepinge the Banner waye untill you come to Norgrove, all Norgrove grounds w[i]thin the Parrish of Feckenham is within auncient Demesne, from thence upp a greene Lane untill you come to trumpe fields bringinge in the same fields ther going forwards unto a house \called/ Poukes Ten[eme]nt soe downe in a Lane called Potters untill you come to Ridialls Oake so up an other Lane unto Gallows Hall goeinge downe unto a howse in the occupac[i]on of one Robert Boulton, then Turne Downe the Lane unto hunt end soe up unto Wadberrowe Hill, all one the right hand still is auncient Demesne, then down a Little lane called Whoomans Lane untill you come to Bowles Fields leaving out Popes Slade and the Birches soe downe another greene Lane bringinge in Mr Cocketts then turninge upp another lane unto the Ridgewaye neere unto Towkeyes place then followinge the Bannerwaye still round about bringinge in all Beanes Hall fields unto Bradley greene Comeinge Downe by Beanehall now unto Rustians Lane and soe Downe the Lane unto Nowers greene againe and there it endeth, and all one the right hand is still auncient Demesne.*

Maps only survive for a small minority of manors. Often a tithe map is the earliest detailed map upon which places found in documents may be located. These usually date from the first half of the nineteenth century and were draw up as part of the administration of the parish, not the manor. Earlier enclosure maps were made between 1709 and the General Inclosure Act of 1845 when a lord wished to enclose open fields, commons and waste. Enclosure maps recording the enclosure of common land were very accurate, but unlike the tithe maps, many only include those areas that were enclosed and do not feature dwellings, villages or unaffected parts of the manor. Stewards used copies of both tithe maps and enclosure maps for their own reference and many nineteenth-century written surveys contain the numbers of plots which correspond with the numbers on the maps. In the twentieth century, plots of copyhold land to be enfranchised were often referenced by the plot numbers on 25-inch Ordnance Survey maps.

Maps of individual tenements were sometimes drawn on nineteenth century copyhold agreements, court rolls and earlier surveys. Those found in copyhold agreements were often based on the tithe survey and provide a clear indication of the land included in a particular tenement which may have retained the same boundaries and structure for several centuries.

Perambulations are the formal record of the boundaries of the manor. Some were compiled at regular events at which the tenants and steward 'beat the bounds' of the manor by physically walking around its perimeter in a ceremony that predated map-making and resulted in a social occasion. Others were carried out by representatives of the homage who were summoned to inspect all or part of the manor boundary when a dispute arose. Occasionally, a water bailiff or port reeve might take to the water to continue a perambulation across a stretch of water, a ceremony that still survives at Poole (Dorset). The steward noted those features which formed the boundary with adjacent manors or estates such as streams or hedges and ensured that any moveable features, such as stones, were correctly positioned. Linked to the perambulations are the presentments in manor court rolls instructing tenants to ensure that marker stones were correctly positioned or for a panel of homagers to inspect boundaries and the placement of boundary markers. A perambulation, extent or boundary survey is often the earliest document that allows us to position a manor on a modern map and it may contain descriptions of features that are no longer visible.

Courts of survey and perambulations developed into social occasions at which the lord provided food and drink and there was an element of ritual, procession and ceremony: they were events designed to bind a community together as well as to fulfil an administrative function. The culmination in a feast or dinner provided by the lord of the manor reinforced community bonds and, particularly on larger manors, brought diverse groups together. Similarly with the celebrations accompanying an end of harvest meal provided by the lord, or the division of meadow in a customary drawing of lots, game or ceremony, these occasions gave the inhabitants of each manor their own distinct identity.

11
The Relationship between Manors and Boroughs

The relationship between manors and boroughs is very complex, and often changed over time. Ancient prescriptive boroughs existed as islands in manorial seas, where the borough institution and community controlled land and exercised jurisdiction within a defined urban jurisdiction (sometimes called a 'banleuca') outside manorial control. These are generally royal boroughs, county towns, and the oldest monastic boroughs. Yet most towns in England and Wales were the product of commercial and institutional innovations after 1100, and their relationship with the manor is more complex. Some boroughs were created across a number of manors; some were late insertions within a single manor; and, finally, some settlements possessed all the economic and social characteristics of a town, but never obtained formal borough status.

Boston provides an example of a major town that first emerged on land belonging to a number of manors, in this case four on both sides of the river Witham. The urban settlement grew across land belonging to the four manors, and each manor held separate courts and markets.[107] Coventry and Durham were also towns with divided administrations. More common were boroughs that were created within a single manor, usually at some time in the late twelfth or thirteenth centuries. In these cases, a lord obtained a royal charter to create a borough within an existing manor, with defined rights for its burgesses to run trade, exchange land, and hold a borough court and market and fair courts independent of the manor. These are often described as mesne boroughs, and they had obtained a degree of formal autonomy to run their affairs from the manor. Yet income from the borough rents, courts and markets are often recorded within the manorial account, reflecting their late insertion into an existing manorial framework.

The third type of town was when a rural manor with a royal grant to hold a weekly market gradually and organically grew and acquired urban functions: in other words, it had become a small market town, with all the economic, social and cultural characteristics of a town, but without any formal borough status or apparatus, such as burgesses, or a borough court, or a borough market court. These manorial market towns were effectively run through the jurisdictional apparatus of the manor, which may have been adapted to deal with the peculiar demands of urban life, such as public order and health issues. As these issues usually fell under the jurisdiction of the Court Leet, then it is often the case that these market towns, such as Braintree and even Manchester, continued to be run through the Court Leet well into the nineteenth centuries. The Court Leet of Loughborough elected a raft of additional officers; streetmasters, pinders, appraisers of the market, aletasters, to run the town. They were assisted by a trust created by the townsfolk in the mid-sixteenth century to look after the bridge in the centre of the town and the school, and by the enhanced powers of the parish under the churchwardens.[108] From the late fifteenth century the new legal institution of incorporation could be

---

107 Rigby, *Boston*, 60-3.

108 Postles, *A town in its parish*, 43-74.

used to provide some of these market towns with the ability to act as a corporate body separate from manorial jurisdiction, although of course this would involve the manorial lord losing some control over an important asset within the manor.

The ancient royal boroughs that had markets before 1066 were generally not part of a manor, having their own autonomous administrations. Nevertheless, even among the four boroughs held by the Crown in Dorset in 1066 there was considerable variation. In Bridport or Dorchester there is no evidence that there was ever a manorial court or lord. Shaftesbury was divided between a royal manor, which held courts until the end of the fifteenth century, and a manor belonging initially to the town's abbey and later to the earls of Shaftesbury which held courts into the late eighteenth century.[109] At Wareham, a single manor passed from the Crown to private hands in the early twelfth century, but fines were imposed by the manor court in 1880 and in 1977, the Criminal Justice Act specifically allowed this court to meet, appoint officers and take presentments relating to commons, the pound and the town's Saxon walls. In both Shaftesbury and Wareham, the manors gradually ceded authority to borough courts.

Villages that had been granted medieval borough charters still held a manor courts which continued to operate when they later developed into larger centres. Birmingham (Warwickshire) was a small manufacturing town at the start of the seventeenth century mostly administered through a manorial Court Leet, and although part of the town was designated a borough from as early as 1250, the leet's officers controlled misbehaviour and nuisances.[110] As the town grew, after 1600 the Court Leet's powers were gradually reduced as control passed to a statutory body of Street Commissions. In 1806 the Street Commissioners farmed the tolls of the market, in all practical ways became the governing authority, and the Court Leet was reduced to an elaborate luncheon.[111] In most places where a medieval manor was replaced by a borough, the transition took place incrementally over hundreds of years as authority was gradually ceded from one institution to the other until any residual rights were finally transferred under the Municipal Corporations Act in 1835.[112]

In an unusually clear cut division between borough and manor at New Alresford (Hampshire), the bishop of Winchester granted the borough a written constitution in 1570 or 1572 making it independent of his manor court.[113] Here the single manor was replaced by a borough court which replaced the Court Leet and created a new borough administration. Like at Arlesford, Chippenham (Wiltshire) received a charter in the mid-sixteenth century. This royal charter of incorporation in granted in 1554 created a new borough administration, but some land within the borough was still part of the two manors of Chippenham and Monkton.[114] Consequently the newly founded borough did not have authority or control over certain infrastructure maintenance and construction projects. Property within the borough held by Chippenham manor partly consisted of small areas of waste or common beside roads; in 1901 a rental of quit rents includes: 10s paid by the Talbot Hotel for the four grates in the pavement that lit basement rooms and 5s

---

109 Hutchins, *The history and antiquities of the county of Dorset*, v.3, 11-15.

110 Stephens (ed.), *The City of Birmingham*, 73-80 and 318-27.

111 Webb and Webb, *English local government*, 157-60.

112 The Municipal Corporations Act 1835 (5 & 6 Wm. IV, c.76).

113 Webb and Webb, *English local government*, 163.

114 Goldney, *Records of Chippenham*.

from the rural sanitary authority for breaking the surface of the road to maintain the water main.[115] The lord of Chippenham manor also tried to exercise his rights to compensation when the General Post Office erected telephone poles in a protracted, and ultimately unsuccessful, dispute finally resolved in the same year.

In Manchester (Lancashire), where a market charter had been granted in 1301, the lord of the manor's Court Baron and Court Leet continued to play a dominant role in the development of the town until 1846. Manchester manor is exceptional in many ways; not least for the survival and publication of records which detail the full functions of offices that elsewhere became absorbed into parish or borough administrations.[116] Here, a well managed manor court and a large range of manorial officers took the lead role in managing the town's affairs. The charter of 1301 had obliged the new burgesses of Manchester to use the lord's mill, malt kiln and oven. The lease of the mill had passed to Manchester Grammar school by 1757, when serious rioting caused by its monopoly within the town brought it to an end, but a tax on the malt kiln was maintained, yielding £2250 in 1825. Control of the market was within the jurisdiction of the officers of the Court Leet and here again there were considerable profits. An officer known as the borough reeve was in effect a head police constable and the burgage tenants were obliged to attend the lord of the manor's Court Leet.[117] The officers appointed by the court dealt with the usual nuisances and regulation found in any larger village such as loose pigs and un-muzzled dogs, but also had to contend with the new industrial problems of excessive factory smoke and the smell of gas-lime.

Manchester manor was profitable, both to the lord and to the group of wealthier inhabitants who served as the leading officers and jurors. Until the middle of the eighteenth century this was an adequate, even efficient, method of running the town. As the population grew, the Manchester Court Leet still appointed only two constables and relied heavily on the inhabitants to form a 'watch', so it could not adequately police what was becoming one of the largest towns in England. In 1765

36. Canford Magna manor, Dorset, 1851.
Oath sworn according to an Act that passed through Parliament during the fifth and sixth years of the reign of Queen Victoria (June 1841-June 1843). A tithingman was appointed at a manor court to enforce legislation which used the parish as its principal administrative unit.

---

115 *Victoria County History, Wiltshire, vol..XX Chippenham* (forthcoming).

116 Earwaker, *The Court leet records of the manor of Manchester.*

117 Webb and Webb, *English local government,* 99-113.

and 1792, acts of Parliament made provision for a body of police commissioners to appoint paid watchmen, light the street and collect a 'police rate'. The police commissioners initially comprised almost exclusively manorial officers, but as the nineteenth century progressed they came to include churchwardens, overseers and surveyor of highways as the town's ruling elite broadened their base. By the 1830s, there arose a popular demand for wider representation, the town's incorporation and the end of the manor court. In 1846 the Town Council purchased the manor with all its rights and incidents for the sum of £200,000.

12
The Changing Functions of Manors and their Courts

At the end of the fifteenth century, manors were already old institutions and their operation was now different from their thirteenth-century antecedents. Over the previous three hundred years the leasing of demesnes, conversion of customary tenures to copyholds, freeholds and leaseholds, use of higher courts for private litigation and shift in responsibilities for local administration from Courts Leet to the parish vestry had gradually eroded the role of the manorial courts. These processes were to continue for the next four hundred years until copyhold tenure and leet jurisdictions were finally abolished. However while the manor in 1600 was already in some respects an archaic survival, and had lost some of it's original regulatory functions, the retreat was slow and certain manor continued to perform important administrative roles.

At the start of the sixteenth century in England and Wales, the manor sat alongside the parish, although more often than not they did not occupy the same geographical area, neither did the manor typically coincide with the normal area used for taxation, the vill.[118] It was the parish vestry, rather than the manorial Court Leet, that was chosen by successive Tudor monarchs to be the institution through which certain new laws would be administered. In addition to its religious functions, the ecclesiastical parish gained responsibility for poor relief from 1552 by various Acts consolidated in 1601 and continued to exercise this secular role until the development of civil parishes in the nineteenth century. Responsibility for the maintenance of highways and the appointment of inspectors also fell to the parish from 1555; these functions were often carried out exclusively by the parish vestry, but in many places the manor court and manorial administration retained an informal role because they had traditionally had some responsibility for these areas. Thus the manor sat alongside the parish, sometimes sharing boundaries and officers, always as separate institutions with clearly defined legal responsibilities. Over several centuries, the administrative boundaries between these parallel administrations might become blurred as people found the easiest ways of managing their communities, but as a general rule it was the manor that gradually ceded authority to the parish.

In other respects, from the start of the sixteenth century, the functions of the manor court declined as the importance of other institutions grew. Besides the parish vestry's acquisition of a more prominent role in the maintenance of

---

118 Kosminsky, *Studies in the agrarian history of England*, 73-5.

parish infrastructure and poor relief, the Quarter Sessions and higher royal courts began to be the places where tenants brought disputes between each other and with their lords. In manors such as Terling (Essex), the manor courts had ceased to have almost any function other than recording land transactions by the start of the sixteenth century, and prosecutions for nuisances were brought before the church courts or Quarter Sessions.[119] However on other manors, the courts remained active bodies as users adapted them to suit changing circumstances. At Bechill (Yorkshire), jurors fined tenants for nuisances such as loose swine and collapsed fences in the early eighteenth century, and the tenants of Whittlesey (Cambridgeshire) used the manor court in 1788 to threaten the churchwardens with fines if they failed to suppress unlawful activities in the alehouses on Sundays.[120]

From the start of the sixteenth century, tenants began to resolve more complex disputes in the courts of common law. At the manor court of Hindringham (Norfolk) in 1539, the tenants had refused to come to a verdict in an action brought by the farmer, Martin Hastings, against a tenant for selling oaks from his holding. Six years later, Hastings brought a case of trespass in the Court of Common Pleas against tenants whom he accused of felling trees on his land. Hastings appears to have believed that he had more chance of success by use of an external court, while the tenants argued that this was an attempt to undermine their customary rights.[121] Tenants might also bring cases against their lords, many town merchants who had purchased customary land in rural manors were used to dealing with central courts, and they must have thought that the cards would be stacked against them in a court held by the lord with whom they were in dispute.

In sixteenth century Wales there was an additional pressure towards a more Anglicised administration. The estate manuals were in English, they principally concerned English laws and English manors, and Welsh manors might be administered by English stewards. In the mid-sixteenth century The Laws of Wales Acts, 1535 and 1542, appear to have had an immediate effect upon some manors.[122] The act of 1535 made English the only language that could be used within the court, and the Act of 1542 abolished the form of partible inheritance called gavelkind, which was known in most regions, but particularly common in Kent and throughout Wales.[123] At Ogmore (Glamorgan), circa 1550, the manorial accounts explicitly relate the decline in the manor's profitability to the introduction of English laws (below). In Nantconwy (North Wales), freeholders and tenants refused to accept Crown manorial rights over wastes and commons, which in some areas led to encroachment, as traditional Welsh methods of regulation broke down.[124]

A considerable body of case law began to be combined with the medieval estate management manuals to provide instructions for stewards. In 1630 Sir Edward Coke, brought together manuals and case law in *The compleate copy-holder* 'wherein is contained a learned discourse of the antiquity and nature of manors and copy-holds, with all things thereto incident, as surrenders, presentments,

---

119 Wrightson and Levine, *Poverty and piety in an English village*, 112.

120 Waddell, 'Governing England through the manor courts', 307-9.

121 Garnett-Goodyear, 'Common law and the manor courts', 49-50.

122 An Acte for Laws & Justice to be ministred in Wales in like fourme as it is in this Realme (27 Henry VIII c. 26), An Acte for certaine Ordinaunces in the Kinges Majesties Domynion and Principalitie of Wales (34 and 35 Henry VIII c. 26).

123 Kerridge, *Agrarian problems in the sixteenth century and after*, 34-5.

124 Richardson, 'The enclosure of commons and wastes in Nantconwy', 49-73.

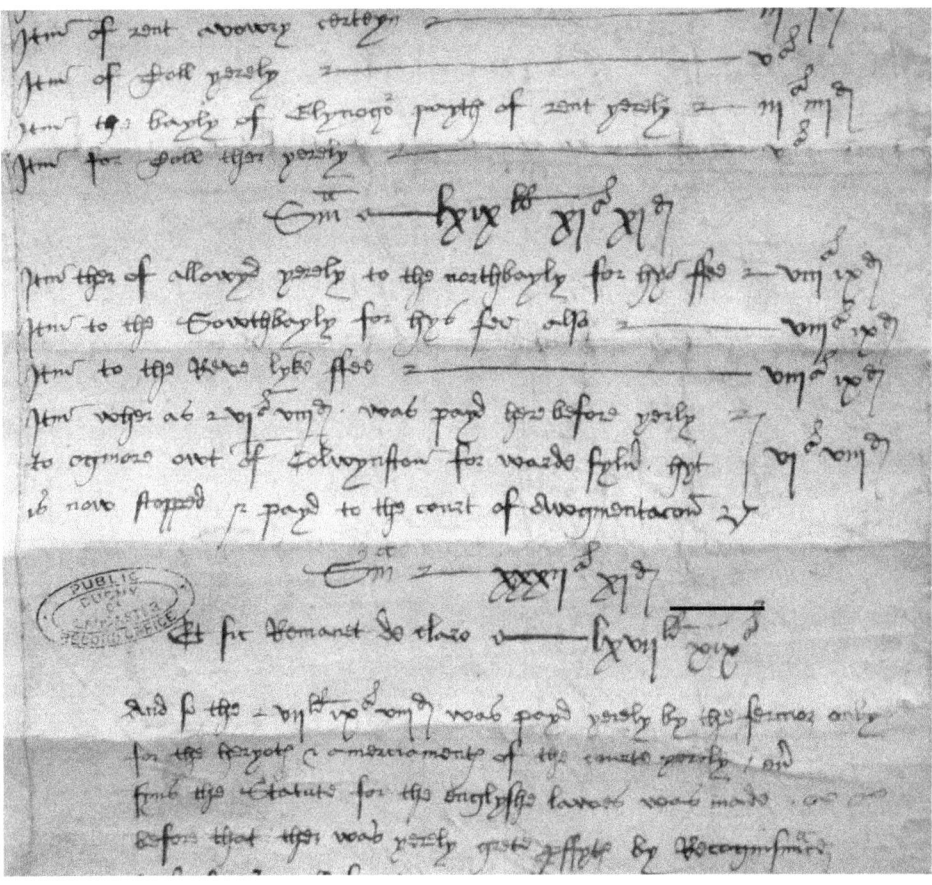

37. Accounts for rents at Ogmore, Glamorgan, circa 1550.

[eight preceding entries]
It[e]m of Toll yerely   vs
It[e]m the bayly of Glynogo[ur] payth of rent yerely   iijs iiijd
It[e]m the Toll ther yerely   vs
    S[u]m[ma]   lxix li xjs xjd

It[e]m ther of allowyd yerely to the northbayly for hys Fee   viijs ixd
It[e]m to the Sowthbayly for hys fee also   viijs ixd
It[e]m to the Reve lyke Fee   viijs ixd
It[e]m wher as vjs viijd was payd here before yerly   }
to ogmore owt of Colwynston for Warde Sylv[er] hyt   }   vjs viijd
is now stopped & payd to the court of Awgmentacon   )
    S[u]m[ma]   xxxijs xjd

Et sic Remanet de claro lxvij li xixs
[and there remains clear]

*And so the vij li ixs viijd was payd yerely by the fermor only
for the heryot[es] & amerciament[es] of the courte yerely ev[er]
syns the Statute for the Englyshe Lawes was made
before that ther was yerely grete p[ro]ffyt[es]by Recognis[a]unces*

admittances, forfeitures, customes, etc. necessary both for the lord and tenant: together, with the forme of keeping a copy-hold court, and Court Baron'. Prior to its publication Coke was successively Speaker of the House of Commons, Solicitor General, Attorney General, Chief Justice of the Common Pleas and Chief Justice of the King's Bench. His manual was a guide to current legal practice by a leading legal figure, not an historical analysis. Further guides followed, always drawing from the earlier texts, until the publication of the final edition of Giles Jacob's *Complete Court Keeper* in 1819. While these manuals encouraged standardisation of procedure, there remained considerable differences between the customs of individual manors and the way in which business was transacted.

From the sixteenth century, some lords began to buy out their copyholders or exchanged their copies for freehold or leasehold agreements, thus removing the conveyancing function from the manor court (see above, section 6). Once the copyholds had been exchanged for leases or sold as freehold, they could not be restored as no legal mechanism existed for new copyholds to be created, so customary tenure gradually disappeared from many manors. The manor court needed to meet with less frequency when tenants began to make out of court transfers of land in the presence of witnesses which might be ratified at a later court; a process initiated on some manors in the mid-fourteenth century, but not adopted on others until the sixteenth century.[125] Although the administration of tenancies required fewer courts, other aspects of estate management still needed to be considered. Copyholders, leaseholders and freeholders might all enjoy some customary rights to common grazing, gathering firewood and allocations of timber for repairs, while the lords continued to exercise their rights to hunting, fishing, minerals, timber the profits of wrecks and holding markets.

Freeholds, copyholds and leases could all be sub-let. How frequently this occurred is very difficult to determine. Freeholders could sub-let without reference to the steward or Court Baron and although customary tenants generally needed

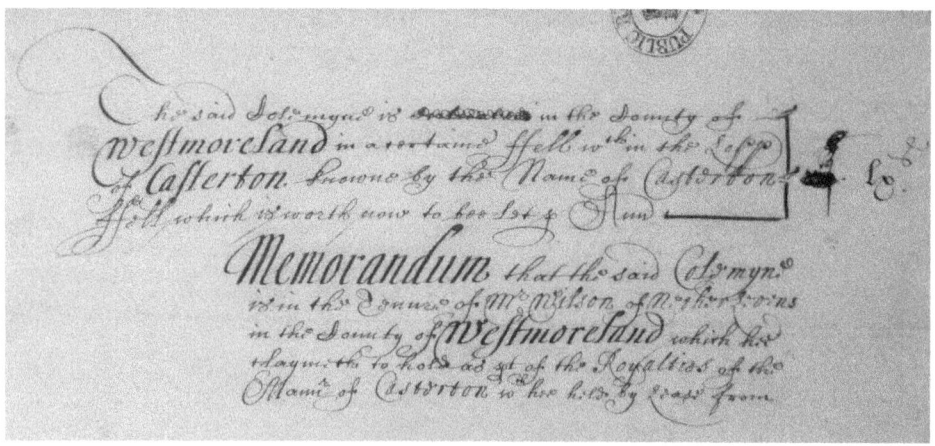

38. Casterton manor, Westmorland, 1652.

The said Cole myne is in the County of Westmoreland in a certaine Fell w[i]thin the Lo[rdshi]pp of Casterton knowne by the Name of Casterton Fell which is worth now to bee let p[er] Ann[um], lxs. Memorandum that the said Cole myne is in the Tenure of Mr Wilson of Nether Levens in the County of Westmoreland which hee claymeth to hold as p[ar]t of the Royalties of the Manno[ur] of Casterton w[hi]ch hee held by Lease from ...

---

125 Bonfield and Poos, 'The development of deathbed transfers', 128.

to seek a licence from the lord to sub-let their holdings in the fifteenth century this requirement was gradually dropped in the sixteenth and seventeenth centuries. At Earls Colne, the customs of the manor allowed tenants to sub-let their copyholds for up to three years without obtaining a licence.[126] As a result, the true extent of sub-tenancies is not immediately apparent from the court rolls, and they might well be obscured in many other early modern manors. At Earls Colne it is possible to reconstruct the 'hidden' structure of sub-tenancies by using the parish rate books, which list both owners and occupiers, in conjunction with the manorial record, which emphasises the important point that complementary sources might be needed to reconstruct the reality of land holding in early modern communities. On this manor more than 40% of the copyhold was sub-tenanted and to some extent it was linked to life-cycle, as young heirs and female heirs were more likely to lease their lands.[127] Only the minority of sub-tenants who were also copyholders were obliged to attend the manor court or hold manorial offices, so many of the resident agriculturalists lost their direct connection with manorial authority: in effect sub-tenancy 'wrecked the manor court'.[128] At Mere (Wiltshire) in the early sixteenth century, the surveyor John Norden found the tenants frequently sub-let for periods of up to 20 years, while pretending that each lease was for one year only. At Cerne Abbas (Dorset) in 1617 Norden complained that larger houses had been sub-let to 'a mass of base people' and that one fine house had 'near a dozen lousy people in it'.[129] Manorial documents remain important sources for reconstructing landholding patterns in early modern communities, but the researcher needs to be aware that the reality of occupation might be very different to ownership due to the increasingly lax recording of sub-tenancies.

The extinguishment of copyholds was sometimes carried out at the same time as the enclosure of common fields. The process of enclosure had begun in some areas in the thirteenth century and was carried out with zeal by new Tudor landlords in the second half of the sixteenth century, gradually spreading to all parts of the country, on some manors with the assent of the tenants and on others with considerable opposition. Between 1709 and the General Inclosure Act of 1845,[130] almost 4,000 individual acts of Parliament enclosed common fields and exchanged property rights, and collections of stewards' papers often provide additional details of the enclosure beyond the terms of the act. Under the Inclosure Acts, the surviving ancient systems of common strip fields, grazing and waste were replaced by the small hedged fields found today and, even on those manors where copyholding survived the process, a significant set of common resources that had been regulated by the customs of the manor disappeared. Stewards of small manors, which held a few strips or sections within a common or open field, found that following enclosure they no longer had to defend their rights against encroachment from the tenants of the principal manor. Enclosure required the consent of the proprietors of four-fifths of the land in the manors that comprise the field. This percentage of those with rights to the commons and customary rights may have been relatively small, but in many areas enclosure was deeply unpopular in the wider community and reflected both in the manor court rolls and the Quarter Sessions. The acts and

---

126 French and Hoyle, *The character of English rural society*', 146.

127 French and Hoyle, *The character of English rural society*', 251-83.

128 French and Hoyle, *The character of English rural society*', 173-4 and 295.

129 Bettey, '"Ancient custom time out of mind", copyhold tenure in the west country', 313-14.

130 The Inclosure Act, 1845 (8 & 9 Vict. c.118).

their accompanying maps are often preserved in the Quarter Sessions records, frequently supplemented by stewards' papers, courts of survey and references in the manor court rolls.

Over several centuries, then, changes such as leasing of the demesnes, acquisition of land by absentees, enclosure of open fields, extinguishment of copyholds, plaintiffs selecting to seek judgements in royal courts and the transfer of regulatory powers to the parish vestry, eroded the functions and purpose of the manor and its courts. By the eighteenth century on some manors the amount of business had shrunk so far that the court was sometimes held only when a copyhold property changed hands, resulting in gaps of several years between sessions of the Court Baron. The functions of the Court Leet, relating to road maintenance, appointment of constables, prosecuting offences and dealing with nuisances were gradually transferred to the parish and higher courts. Across England and Wales, this gradual reduction in the reasons for summoning a manor court meant that they were held less frequently or abandoned altogether. As these changes occurred at different times according to local circumstances, many courts ceased to have a reason to continue during the seventeenth, eighteenth and nineteenth centuries.

Copyhold tenure was abolished by the Law of Property Act 1922 which came into force in 1926.[131] Most of the remaining copyholds were converted to freeholds, with a small number that had been held for terms of years converted to leaseholds. Once the regulatory function for copyhold tenancies had been removed, there was little purpose to the manor courts, although the manors themselves retained some sporting and mineral rights. After the abolition of copyhold tenure, manorial incidents remained in former copyhold land, notably quit and chief rents, fines, reliefs (including forfeiture), heriots, alienation fees, lords' rights to timber and fees payable to stewards. These incidents could be extinguished at any time between 1926 and 1 January 1936 by the payment of compensation by the tenant, agreement or by notice given by the lord. After 1935, incidents were automatically extinguished, but until 1 November 1950, an application could be made to the Ministry of Agriculture and Fisheries to determine whether compensation was payable. Adjudications and agreements between parties are in several series at The National Archives, particularly series MAF 13 and MAF 27, as well as in family and estate records in private collections and county archives.

In order to demonstrate the ownership of rights to land that had formerly been copyhold the Manorial Documents Register was established, under the supervision of the Master of the Rolls, to record the whereabouts of all manorial documents. From 1926, the index of all manorial documents was maintained by the Master of the Rolls, this responsibility passed to the Royal Commission on Historical Manuscripts, known as the Historical Manuscripts Commission (HMC), in 1959 and is now based at the National Archives. The Manorial Documents Rules, a statutory instrument, came into force in 1959 to ensure that manorial documents are listed, kept in appropriate conditions and not removed from the country.[132]

Manorial titles are separate from the physical property of the manor; they had to be registered with Land Registry by 2003, and advice regarding their transfer can be found on the website of the Manorial Society of Great Britain. A small number of courts continue to meet regularly as ceremonial, charitable and occasionally, regulatory bodies to the present day; at Danby (North Yorkshire) the Court Leet

---

131 The Law of Property Act 1922 (12 & 13 Geo. 5 c. 16).

132 The Manorial Documents Rules 1959, SI 1959/1399, amended 1963 (SI 1963/976) and 1967 (SI 1967/963).

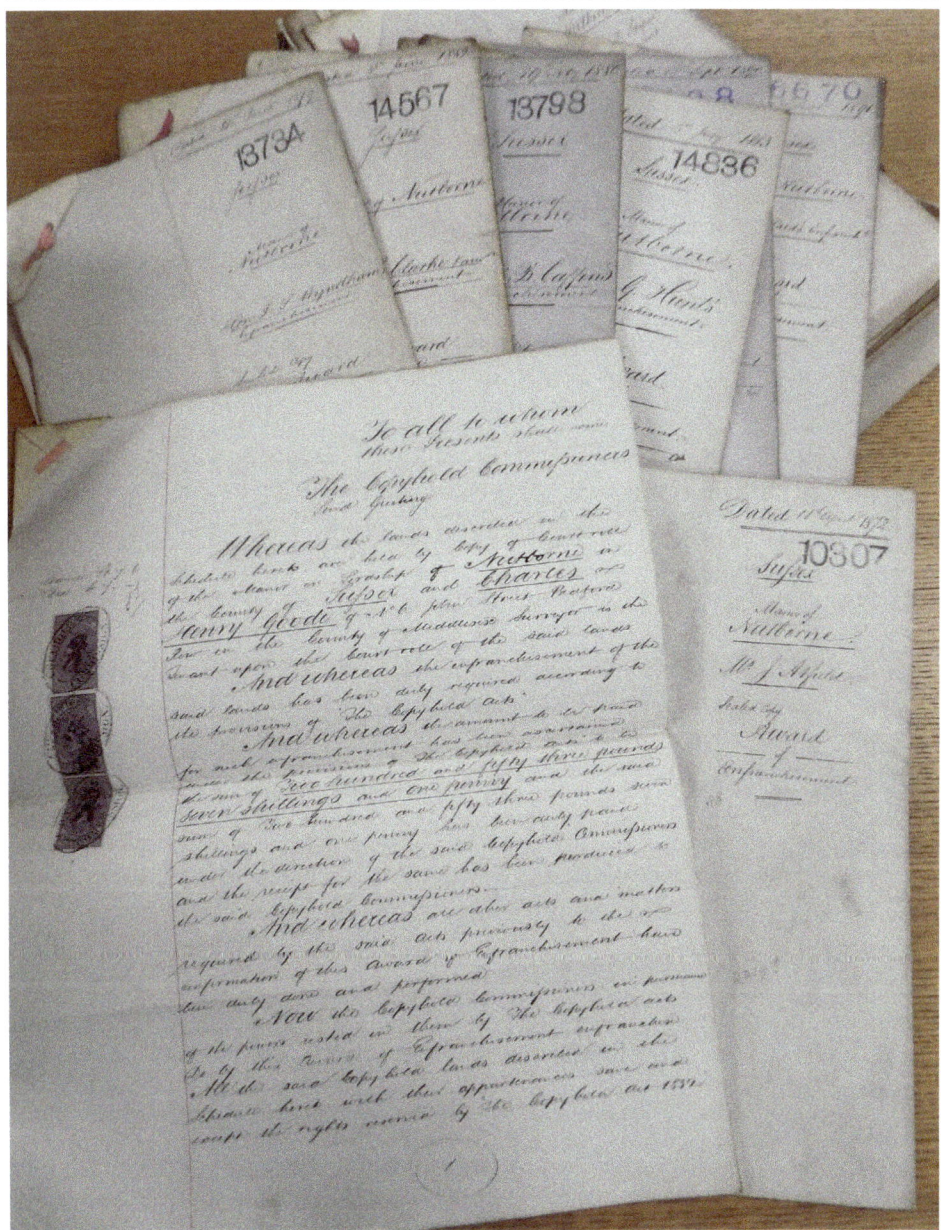

39. A file of papers relating to the enfranchisement of copyhold land, Nutborne manor, Suffolk, 1872-1925

allocates grazing rights on the common land that extends across the moors.[133] The Administration of Justice Act 1977 ordered that manorial courts should cease to hear legal proceedings and carried a schedule of those courts leet and Baron that might still be held and the business they could transact.[134] Other rights remained

---

133 Cookson, 'Danby Court Leet'.

134 The Administration of Justice Act 1977, c.38; part 23, Jurisdiction of Ancient Courts; schedule 4, Curtailment and Jurisdiction of Certain Ancient Courts.

even when the courts ceased to be held. Lords can still exercise their rights to markets, extraction of minerals below the sub-soil and to sporting rights such as fishing where the lord of the manor still has control of the river bank. Under the Land Registration Act of 2002, all manorial rights had to be registered at the Land Registry by 2013, and there is no longer a presumption that any unregistered historical rights remain.[135]

Thus it is apparent from the above discussion that the manor was an essential part of British life for at least a millennium and has left its mark on the nation's cultural heritage in literature, law and landscape of the country. A few manor courts retain some of their original functions; at Laxton (Nottinghamshire), a Court Leet still administers the three open fields in one of the few remaining common field systems in England.[136] Elsewhere they have adopted ceremonial roles; for instance, at Bromsgrove (Worcestershire), the officers of the Court Leet meet regularly to support local businesses, organisations, schools and charities. In the popular culture of London and the south-east, the word 'manor' is still used in the twenty-first century to define the home area of a person and their social group, usually without any knowledge of the origins of the term.

13
Case Studies Appearing in Works using Manorial Documents

Although medievalists have made much more use of manorial documents than historians of the early modern and modern periods, there are some excellent examples of studies using records from those later periods. For local historians unfamiliar with manorial documents it may be useful to see how they have been used with other records to examine different communities.

1. Margaret Spufford, *Contrasting Communities: English villagers in the sixteenth and seventeenth centuries* (Cambridge, first edition 1974, second edition 2000). Spufford examines three Cambridgeshire villages; Chippenham, Orwell and Willingham, each sited in a different geological and economic region through manorial, parish and civil records.

Chippenham, situated on chalk near the Suffolk border, has an extraordinarily detailed manorial survey of 1544, which could be plotted onto a 1712 estate map, a rental dated 1570 and a run of court rolls from the late fourteenth century to 1636 with only small gaps in the sequence. The manorial records are very good, to some extent compensating for the thin series of wills, patchy parish registers and lack of the particularly inclusive taxation assessments from the 1523 lay subsidy. From these records, it is possible to reconstruct a detailed history of land tenure within the manor, examining inheritance patterns, property holding in widowhood and the divisions or agglomeration of holdings.

At Orwell, where the soil is a heavy clay, a survey of the demesne carried out in 1601 may be examined alongside a series of disputes about demesne leases brought to the court of Exchequer in 1605 and a survey of the copyholds carried

---

135 The Land Registration Act 2002, c.9.

136 Beckett, 'Laxton's open fields and Court Leet'.

out in 1607 preliminary to the sale of the manor in 1627 when a second survey was made. A detailed map made in the 1670s, rental of 1675 and survey of 1682 containing some retrospective commentary were used with a good set of parish registers to provide a detailed examination of the changes in distribution of copyholds in the first quarter of the seventeenth century, but a complete absence of court rolls made it impossible to extend the study beyond this period.

The fenland manor of Willingham has a very good series of surveys dated 1575, 1601, with a map, and circa 1720, as well as a terrier from 1603. These documents give the framework to examine a series of disputes relating to enclosure of fenland and common rights which were resolved through successive Chancery cases. The court rolls for the manor do not survive between 1602 and 1614, but those from before and after the main period of dispute were drawn upon for additional material.

From these studies it could be demonstrated that the medieval half-yardland family holdings survived at Willingham where the tenants had access to additional grazing on the fens, whereas at Orwell and Chippenham, these units were no longer economically viable and were joined together to form larger holdings. At Willingham, younger sons could remain on the manor supporting themselves with small bequests of land supplemented by wage labour, while at Orwell and Chippenham, similar bequests were insufficient to support a family. Population movements and inheritance customs appeared to have little effect in any of the manors compared with broader economic trends such as price rises. By combining the manorial records with those of the parishes and higher courts, Spufford is able to generate biographical information for individuals and families and to set them in a social and economic context.

2. At Terling, in Essex, Keith Wrightson and David Levine also used parish, taxation, high court and manorial records to examine a village community in the sixteenth and seventeenth centuries, K. Wrightson and D. Levine, *Poverty and piety in an English village: Terling*, 1525-1700 (Oxford, first edition 1979, second edition 1995).

Terling was divided between five manors: Terling Place, Ridley Hall, Terling Hall, Ringers, all with demesne, copyhold and freehold land, and Ockendon Fee, which consisted entirely of freeholds. The available documents for each manor varied considerably: for Terling Place a rental dated 1475, a map and survey 1597, court book,1609-1613, rents circa 1650, and rental 1692; Ockendon Fee also had court rolls and books 1581-1719 and several rentals 1632-1715; for Ridley Hall there are court rolls 1675-1681, a rental 1677-1678, and a late seventeenth century survey; but for Ringers there are only court rolls 1698-1705 and for Terling Hall, only a rental of 1722.

The presence of multiple manors within the same parish is not uncommon in Essex and elsewhere and the lack of coincidence for the records of the different manors within a parish is all too typical. However, by piecing together the evidence from the different documents it was possible to establish that in the parish as a whole approximately 16% of the land was freehold, 9% copyhold and the remainder divided between the demesnes with over half belonging to Terling Place where it was leased as five large farms. An examination of the changing roles of these three different types of holdings reveals that the leases generally attracted a market rent, freeholds paid negligible fixed rents but large entry fines and across the manors copyholders paid below market rents with some retaining harvest work services. Some tenants held land in different manors, for example, William Burchard held five acres of freehold and two acres of copyhold in Ridley Hall and also one and a half acres of freehold in Ockendon Fee, this was a situation that occurred across the county and Wrightson and Levine remark upon the difficulty of analysing these cross manorial holdings even within the same parish.

The Terling study reveals that an increasing proportion of the non-demesne land moved from peasants to the gentry who then sub-let it to resident villagers, with most of the change taking place in the first three decades of the seventeenth century. Transfer of freehold and copyhold land was between family members in around half of all transactions and only two freeholds and one copyhold remained in the same family in 1700 as had held them in 1600.

Beyond the tenurial changes, some analysis may be made of those tenants who held manorial offices, or served as jurors in the manor court, compared with those who were overseers of the poor, churchwardens, vestrymen or jurymen at the Quarter Sessions. The results are inconclusive as the tenants were divided between five manors, had relatively few copyholders and by the seventeenth century the manor courts were held irregularly and dealt almost exclusively with conveyancing, but for an earlier period or for a different set of manors this could be more revealing.

3. Another Essex study, covering a slightly earlier period, is by Marjorie Keniston McIntosh, *A community transformed: the manor and liberty of Havering*, 1500-1620 (Cambridge, 1991). The Havering manor court rolls survive for the whole period examined here and as in the other examples, the manorial records are compared with parish records, taxation assessments, wills and higher courts to discuss the whole community.

McIntosh devotes a whole chapter to the decline of the manor court over this period detailing the decrease in number and variety of private suits brought by the tenants. She also observes the decline in public business, such as presentments by the homage on public nuisances, encroachments on common land and maintenance of ditches and roads. Sometimes the responsibility for dealing with a particular issue can be seen to have passed to another authority, such as the maintenance of roads becoming part of the role of parish vestries, or the trial of felonies passing to the Justices of the Peace or higher courts. As the business of the courts declined so did the number and role of its officers: the two marsh reeves, who had been active in earlier courts, ceased to be appointed by the 1590s, and the appointments of other officers became concentrated in a narrow band of wealthier tenants.

Much of the interest in Havering's courts in the sixteenth century lies in charting their decline as a regulator body as the parish and other courts increased their roles. Despite this, certain aspects of the court still functioned and were essential to the community: conveyancing was still managed through the courts, indeed the number of inheritances recorded in the court increased over the period, it continued to manage stray livestock, appointed some officers and had a role in public regulation.

These three studies raise questions about how representative the selected manors are of the local, regional or national situation. Each explores different, but overlapping, aspects of social, economic, demographic and religious change. Some studies have been controversial. Alan Macfarlane's *Reconstructing Historical Communities* (Cambridge, 1977) was one of the first historical studies to use databases analysed by a computer and the resulting study of Earls Colne, Essex, *The Origins of English Individualism* (Oxford, 1978) was not generally well received. Despite for the first time being able to sort tens of thousands of pieces of data from parish registers, taxation records, manorial surveys, rentals and courts, there were methodological problems in the treatment and interpretation of the evidence which have informed subsequent studies.[137] The manor was re-assessed by Henry French and Richard Hoyle in a series of articles and *The Character of English Rural Society, Earls Colne, 1550-1750* (Manchester, 2007) which includes a particularly clear reflection on how sub-letting might undermine the functions of the manorial court.

All these studies use some combination of manorial, parish, probate, taxation and central court records to develop a broad picture of their different communities. Over time, some regulatory functions passed from the manor to the parish or to the other courts in processes that are in themselves the subject of debate and which occurred according to local conditions at different times. The use of manorial documents in the analyses of these villages in the sixteenth, seventeenth and eighteenth centuries enables an exploration of aspects of regulation, office holding, landholding, family relationships and economic changes that would not be possible through other records.

14
The Manorial Documents Register and Access to Documents

The Manorial Documents Register was established by the Master of the Rolls in 1926 to ensure that all manorial documents could be traced should they be required as evidence in legal cases. The Register includes all documents that have statutory protection under the Manorial Documents Rules, defining them as:

> Court rolls, surveys, maps, terriers, documents and books of every description relating to the boundaries, wastes, customs or courts of the manor, but it does not include the deeds or other instruments required for evidencing the title of a manor or agreements or draft agreements relating to compensation, or any documents that came into being after 31st December 1925.

This broad definition is taken to include all those rentals, custumals, perambulations, and other such documents that are not specifically mentioned. Although evidences of title such as deeds, leases, grants and charters are specifically excluded, they are often kept within collections that contain manorial documents and can be found through archival catalogues rather than the Manorial Documents Register. The owners of manorial documents are obliged to ensure that they are listed on the Register, and that they are kept in appropriate secure and climate-controlled conditions. All manorial documents should be listed on the Manorial Documents Register, which may be accessed via the website of The National Archives. For counties in England and Wales, it is possible to search known manorial documents and obtain a comprehensive list of the surviving documents of any type for any manor, wherever the documents are located.[138]

---

137 For criticism of Macfarlane's thesis see for instance Sreenivasan 'The land-family bond at Earls Colne', 3-37. For the continued use of the Earls Colne data to examine changes in land holding French and Hoyle, *The character of English rural society* and French and Hoyle, 'English Individualism refuted: and reasserted'.

138 Links to the Manorial Documents rules and a summary of their contents: https://www.nationalarchives.gov.uk/information-management/legislation/other-archival-

The Manorial Documents Register only lists those documents that fall within the definition under the Manorial Documents Rules. This means that a range of documents, such as copyhold agreements and estate surveys, that relate to the manor but do not fall within the rules are not included in the Register. Fortunately, these documents usually form part of collections that contain other documents which are included, so that it is always worth looking at the rest of the contents of a collection's catalogue when it is found to contain some manorial documents. Archivists compiling the Manorial Documents Register did not have the opportunity to examine every document and often relied upon the descriptions provided from existing catalogues, usually only checking the manuscripts for clarification. After a hundred years of cataloguing in archive offices and muniment rooms across the country, there are some inconsistencies, the most common apparently arising from archivists' use of a document's own heading to describe the contents. This process may have led to cataloguing of copies of court roll as 'Court Leet with view of frankpledge', and no differentiation between rentals, rent rolls, surveys and perambulations. Some of these anomalies have been noted by the project officers working on the computerised version of the Manorial Documents Register.

The Manorial Documents Register is not a register of lordships: these are registered with Land Registry. Claims to rights held by manorial lords had to be registered with Land Registry under the Land Registration Act 2002 and any rights that have not now been registered are not presumed to be current. Ownership of a manorial lordship does not mean that a lord may make any claim to manorial documents that are not already in their possession.

Access to most documents depends upon the policies of the institution where they are held. As a rough guide, approximately half of the documents for each county will be held in collections within that county's archive or record office, a quarter at The National Archives and the British Library, and a quarter scattered throughout the archives of other institutions and in private collections. Of this final quarter, some may be held by university or school archives, others in the archives of other counties. Many Oxford and Cambridge colleges were endowed with manors in the Middle Ages and frequently acquired others at the Dissolution. Similarly larger public schools like Eton, Winchester and Sherborne derive some of their income from endowments of manors. When a landowner places their estate archive in the custody of a county archive, the collection is not broken up, but remains as a complete estate collection. Therefore, a large estate collection deposited in Suffolk is quite likely to contain manorial documents relating to manors in Norfolk, Essex and Hertfordshire, but may also hold documents for manors from Cumbria to Cornwall. A small number of documents are in private collections not available for public consultation and some private owners charge a fee to cover the costs of cataloguing their records, making copies and supervising researchers.

For many years the Manorial Documents Register was maintained as a paper index at the Historic Manuscripts Commission in Chancery Lane. A comprehensive review of its contents and transformation to an online searchable database began with a pilot project on the documents for Pembrokeshire, and the whole of Wales was completed in 1996. The English counties were added gradually over the following two decades with the final county, Cornwall, completed in 2022.

The online Manorial Documents Register is now hosted by The National Archives and researchers may search by manor name, parish, county, keyword and document type. Searches may be refined by date range, so a broad range of searches is possible:

---

legislation/manorial-documents/

Example 1: A search for Chippenham (Wiltshire) reveals seven different manors of which six have surviving manor court rolls.

Example 2: A search for customs in Norfolk reveals 15 documents, 12 at the Norfolk Record Office, two at Holkham Hall in the Earl of Leicester's archive and one at the British Library.

Example 3: a search for manorial documents produced in the eighteenth century relating to mines reveals 46 entries for records held in The National Archives, The National Library of Wales, Sheffield City Archives, Somerset Heritage Centre, Cumbria Archives and Local Studies Centre, West Yorkshire Archives Service, West Glamorgan Archive Service and two private collections.

Select Bibliography

Guides to manors and manorial documents
Bailey, M., *The English manor c.1200 – c.1500* (Manchester, 2002).
Ellis, M., *Using manorial records* (Public Records Office Readers Guide, 1997).
Forrest, M., *Dorset manorial documents: a guide for local and family historians* (Dorset Record Society, 2011).
Harvey, P.D.A, *Manorial records*, revised edition (British Records Association, 1999).
Stuart, D., *Manorial records* (Phillimore, 2005).
Watt, H., *Welsh manors and their records* (National Library of Wales, 2000).
Webb, S. and Webb, B., *English local government from the Revolution to the Municipal Corporations Act: the manor and the borough* (London, 1906).

Select publications for interpreting Latin, handwriting and dates
Cheney, C. R., *Handbook of dates for students of English history*, revised edition (Cambridge, 2000).
Forrest, M., *Reading early handwriting, 1500-1700* (Macclesfield, 2019).
Gooder, E. A., *Latin for local history, an introduction* (London, 1978).
Hector, L. C., *The handwriting of English documents* (Dorking, 1980).
James, K., *English palaeography and manuscript culture, 1500-1800* (Yale, 2020).
Stuart, D., *Latin for local and family historians* (Chichester, 1995).

Other publications mentioned in the text
Bailey M., 'The transformation of customary tenures in southern England, c.1350-c.1500', *Agricultural History Review* (2014), v.62, 210-30.
Beckett, J., 'Laxton's open fields and Court Leet', *Local History News*, (2013) no. 106.
Bettey, J., '"Ancient custom time out of mind", copyhold tenure in the west country in the sixteenth and seventeenth centuries.' *The Antiquaries Journal* (2009), v.89, 307-22.
Birrell, J., 'Manorial custumals reconsidered' *Past and Present*, (2014), v.224, pp.8-9. (whole article, pp.3-37).
Bolton, D. K., King, H. P. F., Wyld G., and Yaxley, D. C., 'Ruislip: Manors and other estates', in Baker, T. F. T., Cockburn, J. S. and Pugh, R. B. (eds.), *A History of the County of Middlesex: Volume 4, Harmondsworth, Hayes, Norwood with Southall, Hillingdon with Uxbridge, Ickenham, Northolt, Perivale, Ruislip, Edgware, Harrow With Pinner*, (London, 1971).

Bonfield L., and Poos, L. R. , 'The development of deathbed transfers', in Z. Razi and R. Smith (eds.) *Medieval society and the manor court*, (Oxford, 1996), 117-42.

Brooks, C., 'The agrarian problem in revolutionary England', in J. Whittle (ed.), *Landlords and tenants in Britain, 1440-1660: Tawney's 'Agrarian Problem' revisited* (Woodbridge, 2013), 183-99.

Campbell, B.M.S., *English seigniorial agriculture, 1250-1450* (Cambridge, 2000).

Campbell, B.M.S., 'The agrarian problem in the early fourteenth century', *Past and Present* (2005), v.188, 1-70.

Campbell, B.M S. and Bartley, K., *England on the even of the Black Death: an atlas of lordship, land and wealth, 1300-1349* (Manchester, 2006).

Collinson, J., *History and Antiquities of the County of Somerset*, 3 vols. (Bath, 1791).

Cookson, G., 'Danby Court Leet', *Local History News*, (2013), no. 107.

Cross, C., 'The economic problems of the See of York: decline and recovery in the sixteenth century', *Land, church and people: essays presented to Professor H. P. R. Finberg*, ed. J. Thirsk, *Agricultural History Review* (1970), v.18, supplement, 64-82.

Crowley, D., *The Court Records of Brinkworth and Charlton, 1544-1648*, (Chippenham, 2009), Wiltshire Record Society, v.61.

Currie, C.R.J., 'Tenants' copies of court rolls in England and Wales before 1400', *Archives* (2021), v.56, 1-21.

Dodd, K. M., *The field book of Walsham-le-Willows, 1577*, (Ipswich, 1974), Suffolk Record Society, v.17.

Dyer, C., 'Peasant holdings in West Midlands villages, 1400-1540' in R. M. Smith (ed.) *Land, Kinship and Lifecycle* (Cambridge, 1984), 277-94.

Dyer, C., *Hanbury: settlement and society in a woodland landscape* (Leicester, 1991).

Earwaker, J. P., *The Court leet records of the manor of Manchester, from the year 1552 to the year 1686, and from the year 1731 to the year 1846*, 12 vols. (Manchester, 1884-90).

Eyre, S. R., 'The curving plough strip and its historical implications', *Agricultural History Review* (1955), v.3, 80-94.

Falvey, H., ed., *Humphry Repton and his family: Correspondence, 1805-1816* (Norfolk Record Society, v.84, 2020).

Forrest, M., Halling Barnard, J., Mitchell R. and Papworth, M., *Ralph Treswell's survey of Sir Christopher Hatton's lands in Purbeck, 1585-6*, (Dorchester, 2017), Dorset Record Society, v.19.

Fraser, C. M. and Emsley, K., *The Court rolls of the manor of Wakefield, 1639-1640*, (Leeds, 1977), Wakefield Court Rolls series volume 1 (see below for series details).

French, H. R., 'Urban agriculture, commons and commoners in the seventeenth and eighteenth centuries: the case of Sudbury, Suffolk', *Agricultural History Review* (2000), v..48, 171-99.

French, H. R., 'Urban common rights, enclosure and the market: Clitheroe town moors, 1764-1802', *Agricultural History Review* (2003), v.51, 40-68.

French, H. R., and Hoyle, R. W., '*English Individualism* refuted: and reasserted: the land market of Earls Colne (Essex), 1550-1750' *Economic History Review* (2005), v. 56, 595-622.

French, H. R., and Hoyle, R. W., *The character of English rural society: Earls Colne, 1550-1750* (Manchester, 2007).

Gage, J., *The history and antiquities of Suffolk: Thingoe hundred* (London, 1838).

Garnett-Goodyear, H., 'Common law and the manor courts: lords, copyholders and doing justice in early Tudor England' in J. Whittle (ed.), *Landlords and tenants in Britain, 1440-1660: Tawney's 'Agrarian Problem' revisited* (Woodbridge, 2013), 35-51.

Goldney, F. H., *Records of Chippenham relating to the borough*, (London, 1889).

Griffiths M., 'Manor court records and the historian: Penmark, Fonmon and Barry, 1570-1622' *Morgannwg* (1981), v.25, 43-78.
Hall, D., *The open fields of England* (Oxford, 2014).
Harvey, B. F., 'The life of the manor', in A. Williams (ed.), *Domesday Book Studies* (London, 1987), 39-42.
Hervey, J., *Ickworth Survey Boocke, anno 1665: Surveyed, and Layed Downe in a Mapp, by Thomas Covell*, (Ipswich, 1893).
Hine, R., *The history of Beaminster* (Taunton, 1914).
Homans, G. D., *English villagers in the thirteenth century* (Harvard, 1941).
Hutchins, J., *The history and antiquities of the county of Dorset*, (Dorchester, third edition reprint, 1974).
Jessel, C., *The law of the manor* (Chichester, 1998).
Jewell, H. M., *English local administration in the middle ages* (Newton Abbot, 1972).
Kanzaka, J., 'Villein rents in thirteenth century England: an analysis of the Hundred Rolls of 1279-80', *Economic History Review* (2002), N.S. v.55, 593-618.
Kanzaka, J., 'Manorialisation and demographic pressure in medieval England: an analysis of the Hundred Rolls of 1279-1280', *Journal of Historical Geography* (2018), v.60, 11-23.
Kerridge, E., *Surveys of the manors of Philip, earl of Pembroke and Montgomery, 1631-2*, Wiltshire Record Society, v.9 (1953).
Kerridge, E., *Agrarian problems in the sixteenth century and after* (London, 1969).
Kosminsky, E.A., *Studies in the agrarian history of England in the thirteenth century* (Oxford, 1956).
Lawton, G., *Church Lawton manor court rolls, 1631-1830*, Lancashire and Cheshire Record Society, v.143 (2013).
McIntosh, M. K., *A community transformed: the manor and liberty of Havering, 1500-1620* (Cambridge, 1991).
McIntosh, M. K., *Controlling misbehaviour in England, 1370-1600*, Cambridge, 1998).
Morrin J., 'Transfer of leasehold on Durham cathedral estate, 1541-1626', in J. Whittle (ed.), *Landlords and tenants in Britain, 1440-1660: Tawney's 'Agrarian Problem' revisited* (Woodbridge, 2013), 117-32.
Nelson, W., *Lex maneriorum: or, the law and customs of England, relating to manors and lords of manors, their stewards, deputies, tenants and others* (London, 1733).
Oothuizen, S., 'The Anglo-Saxon kingdom of Mercia and the origins and distribution of common fields' *Agricultural History Review* (2008), v.55, 153-80.
Oschinsky, D., *Walter of Henley and Other Treatises on Estate Management and Accounting* (Oxford, 1971).
Palmer, J., *Three Tudor Surveys, the manors of Sir Thomas Kitson: Okeford Fitzpaine, Durweston cum Knighton and Lytchett Minster, 1584-1585*, Dorset Record Society, (2015) v.18.
Postles, D., *A town in its parish. Loughborough, origins to c.1640* (Loughborough, 2015).
Razi Z., and Smith R., (eds.) *Medieval society and the manor court*, (Oxford, 1996).
Richardson, F., 'The enclosure of commons and wastes in Nantconwy, North Wales, 1550-1900' *Agricultural History Review* (2017), v.65, 49-73.
Richardson H. G. and Sayles G. O., *Fleta* (Selden Society Publications, v.72, 1955; v.89, 1972; v.99, 1983).
Rigby, S. H., *Boston, 1086-1225. A medieval boom town* (Society of Lincolnshire History and Archaeology, 2017).
Rogers, M., 'Introduction to the manorial system in Wales' in H. Watt, *Welsh manors and their records* (Aberystwyth, 2000), 1-55.
Schofield, P. R., 'The late medieval view of frankpledge and the tithing system: an

Essex case study', in Z. Razi and R. Smith (eds.) *Medieval society and the manor court*, (Oxford, 1996), 408-49.

Shannon, W. D., 'Risks and rewards of wasteland enclosure', in J. Whittle (ed.), *Landlords and tenants in Britain, 1440-1660: Tawney's 'Agrarian Problem' revisited* (Woodbridge, 2013), 150-65.

Spufford, M., *Contrasting communities: English villagers in the sixteenth and seventeenth centuries* (2nd ed., Stroud, 2000).

Sreenivasan, D. G., 'The land-family bond at Earls Colne (Essex), 1550-1650' *Past and Present* (1991), v.131, 3-37

Stacy, N. E., *The charters and custumals of Shaftesbury Abbey, 1089-1216*, (Oxford, 2006).

Stephens, W. B. (ed.), *A History of the County of Warwick: Volume 7, the City of Birmingham*, (Victoria County History, London, 1964).

Tawney, R. H., 'The rise of the gentry: a postscript' *Economic History Review* (1954), n.s. v.7, 91-7.

Thorold Rogers, J. E., *Six centuries of work and wages: the history of English labour* (London, 15th edition, 1923)

Waddell, B., 'Governing England through the manor courts, 1550-1850' *The Historical Journal*, (2012), v.55, 279-315.

Whittle, J., *The development of agrarian capitalism: land and labour in Norfolk, 1440-1580* (Oxford, 2000).

Whittle, J., (ed.), *Landlords and tenants in Britain, 1440-1660: Tawney's 'Agrarian Problem' revisited* (Woodbridge, 2013).

Whittle J., and Yates M., '"Pays reel" ou "pays legal"?: Contrasting patterns of land tenure and social structure in eastern Norfolk and western Berkshire, 1450-1600' *Agricultural History Review* (2000), v.48, 1-26.

Wrightson K., and Levine, D., *Poverty and piety in an English village: Terling, 1525-1700* (Oxford, second edition 1995).

The Manorial Documents Register is located on The National Archives website with the text of the Manorial Documents Rules and a list of the range of manorial documents.
https://discovery.nationalarchives.gov.uk/manor-search

The Yorkshire Archaeological and Historical Society produced six volumes of the Wakefield court rolls in their main series between 1901 and 1945 before establishing a separate series in which a further 19 volumes have been published. The 25 volumes contain documents from within the period 1274-1813 with each volume covering up to 24 years of courts
https://www.yas.org.uk/Publications/Wakefield-Court-Rolls-Series.

Most county archives have produced online guides to their local collections. These often include a list of local published manorial documents or a brief guide to manorial documents in their county. The Lancashire online guide is particularly detailed and contains a useful glossary of regional terms.
https://lancashiresarchives.files.wordpress.com/2016/07/guide-to-lancashire-manorial-records-final.pdf

Glossary

Affeerers or assessors: Senior members of the homage usually appointed in pairs to set the rate of fines and amercements imposed at the manor court.
Amercement: Penalty paid for infringement of by-laws.
Appurtenances: A catch-all term for yards, barns and outbuildings attached to a property.
Assart: A piece of land enclosed from a wood or other uncultivated land.
Bailiff: An officer of the manor court usually an employee of the lord of the manor.
Beadle: An officer of the manor court, usually selected from among the tenants and holding office for one year.
Borough English: Inheritance of customary land by the youngest son (ultimogeniture). Common in Surrey, Middlesex and Sussex, but isolated examples found throughout southern and midland England.
Bovate: The Latin form of 'Oxgang' and a common northern equivalent of the virgate (qv) A variable area of land, sufficient to support a large family, based upon the amount of land that would be ploughed by a team of oxen. The customary holding of wealthier tenants.
Cartbote: The right of a tenant to take trees from common areas to repair farm vehicles, ploughs etc.
Chevage: A payment made by villein tenants for the right to reside outside the manor of their birth.
Copyhold: Land held at the will of the lord and by the customs of the manor. The tenant received a copy of the entry on the manor court roll in which their admission into the tenement was recorded.
Court Baron: Manorial court that might be held as often as every three weeks, but usually less frequently, which all customary tenants were obliged to attend.
Court leet: Manorial court held once or twice each year, attended by all tenants, often involving a view of frankpledge.
Demesne: The part of the manor retained by the lord as a 'home farm'. Either worked by an appointed official, or leased for an annual payment.
Deodand: The lord of the manor's right to claim an item (usually a weapon) which had caused serious injury or death? to one of his tenants.
Distraint: Seizure of property as a sanction to ensure compliance with the orders of the court or to recoup an unpaid fine.
Entry fine: Sum, usually in cash not in kind, paid on the entry of a customary tenant into a tenement, messuage or other landholding.
Escheat: Reversion of property to the lord when there were no further heirs.
Essoin: An apology for absence from a court of a named individual made by another tenant or the whole homage.
Estovers: collective term for the rights of tenants to take wood or timber for fuel and repairs.
Estreat: A summary of the money collected in fines and amercements at a court.
Fee simple: Freehold tenure in which the owner has absolute right to a property.
Ferling: a quarter of a virgate, not to be confused with furlong (an eighth of a mile).
Firebote: The right to take under wood for fuel.
Gavelkind: Form of partible inheritance of customary land common in Kent.
Hedgebote: Right of tenant to take trees from common areas to repair hedges and fences.
Heriot: Sum, usually in kind not in cash, paid on the death of customary tenants

who held land. A form of death duty.

Homage: The sum of all tenants owing fealty to the lord of the manor and obliged to attend his courts.

Hundred: a geographic division of a county, comprising several vills or townships often used as an area for tax assessment.

Hundred court; a royal court which held the view of frankpledge and presided over offences more serious than those tried at the Court Leet and less serious than those heard at Quarter Sessions.

Incidents: Rights to exploit resources upon the manor such as hunting, fishing, minerals, wrecks and fairs.

Manumission: The process by which unfree tenants were granted their freedom.

Merchet: A payment made when a villein's daughter married.

Messuage: A house and grounds.

Oxgang: see **Bovate**

Pannage: A payment made for the right to fatten pigs on acorns and beech mast in the lord's woods for a period of six weeks between Michaelmas (29 September) and Martinmas (11 November).

Presentment: Item brought before the manor court for consideration.

Purpresture: An enclosed piece of property, usually a strip of land beside a road or brought into cultivation from a common or wood.

Quarter days: The four days at which rents were usually payable: the feasts of Michaelmas, Christmas, Lady Day and St John the Baptist (29 September, 25 December, 25 March and 24 June).

Quit rent: A rent paid in lieu of work services.

Relief: Sum, usually in cash not in kind, paid on the entry of a free tenant into a tenement, messuage or other landholding.

Reeve: An officer of the manor, usually selected from among the tenants

Socage manor: A manor held in return for cash or customary payments, not in return for military service.

Steward: An administrator employed by the lord of the manor to manage his estate and preside over his courts and to supervise employees and officers of the court.

Tenement: The land held by a tenant.

View of frankpledge: A right granted by the king to summon all free and villein tenants, to an assembly once, or twice per annum. Usually held at the Court Leet or hundred court.

Virgate: A variable area of land measured in acres (hence the English yardland), sufficient to support a large family, which was the customary holding of wealthier tenants, southern equivalent of the northern bovate (qv) or oxgang.

Yardland: see **Virgate**.

Some Key Dates

1250s: earliest surviving manorial documents.

1306: earliest known manorial copyhold.

1400s: copyhold tenure becomes the most common form of customary tenure.

1535 and 1542: The Laws of Wales Acts, made English the language of legal administration in Wales and abolished certain forms of tenure.

1540s: manors formerly owned by monasteries begin to be redistributed among gentry families and courtiers.

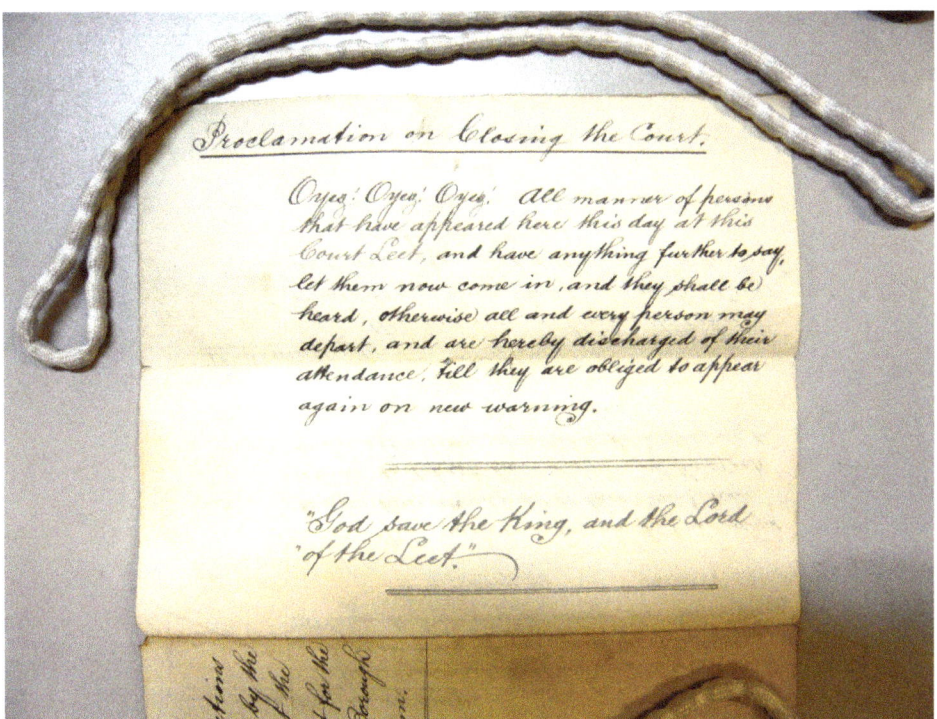

40. The proclamation on closing Wareham manor court, 1900:
Oyez! Oyez! Oyez! All manner of persons that have appeared here this day at this Court Leet, and have anything further to say, let them now come in, and they shall be heard, otherwise all and every person may depart, and are hereby discharged of their attendance, till they are obliged to appear again on new warning."
God save the King and the Lord of the Leet.

1550s onwards: many steward's papers, rentals and surveys compiled in English rather than Latin.
1560s: earliest manorial maps, although these did not become common for a further century.
1650s: all official proceedings of the manor court recorded in English during the Commonwealth, 1649-1660, but revert to Latin at the Restoration.
1730, Proceedings in Courts of Justice Act: made the use of English in all courts obligatory, enforced from 1733.
1845, General Inclosure Act: marked the end of private enclosures.
1852, Copyhold Act: allowed tenants to demand enfranchisement and the conversion of copyhold to freehold.
1876, Commons Act: stated that all enclosures should benefit the neighbourhood rather than just the majority of landholders. This effectively ended enclosure of common land.
1922, Law of Property Act: abolished copyhold tenure.
1924, Law of Property (Amendment) Act: made the Master of the Rolls superintendent of manorial documents.
1926, publication of the Manorial Documents Rules (revised 1959, amended 1963 and 1967).
1977, Administration of Justice Act: prevented courts leet and Baron from making legal decisions and the business that the court might transact.

2003: last date at which titles to manorial lordship could be registered with Land Registry.
2013: last date by which manorial incidents could be registered with Land Registry.
2022: date of completion of work on the online Manorial Documents Register.

Photograph Acknowledgements

Cumbria Archive and Local Studies Centre
Image 6 (D.Cu/2/4)

Dorset History Centre:
Images 2 (D-RWR/M/4), 7 (D-PIT/M/71), 12 (D/FSI/Box12/2a), 13 (D-PIT/T/752), 16 (D-BKL/E/A/3/1/2), 21 (D-FSI/Box286), 25 (D-PIT/Acc9202/1/9), 26 (D-FSI/box12/1d), 30 (D-FSI/box12/1a), 36 (D1/OO/8), 40 (D-RWR/M/4

East Sussex Record Office
Image 28 (BAT 114)

Kresen Kernow
Images 19 (ME/1554) and 34 (AD332/1)

The National Archives.
Images 5 (DL/43/13/11), 15 (MAF9/211/Norfolk), 17 (PRO/30/26/67), 37 (DL/43/13/3), 38 (E317/Westmorland/4), 39 (MAF9/346)

The National Library of Wales
Image 8 (MS 7013E)

Northamptonshire Record Office
Images 4 and 10 (LH.272).

Oxfordshire History Centre
Image 9 (Saye/I/i/21)

Powys Archives
Image 29 (M-BLFBO)

Lord Shaftesbury's Estate Archive, Wimborne St Giles
Images 11 (M147), 18 (ES/216), 20 (M/218), 22 (M42), 31 (ES/182), 32 (P127), 33 (P128)

Staffordshire Record Office
Image 14 (D[W]1553)

Wiltshire and Swindon History Centre
Images 24 (865/325), 27 (473/55)

Worcestershire Archive and Archaeology Service
Images 3 (705:73 BA14450/241/5), 35 (705:73/BA 14450/185)

Index

Adderbury, Oxfordshire, 15
Administration of Justice Act, 1977, 41, 79, 91
Affpuddle manor, Dorset, 51
Alverthorpe, in Wakefield manor, 10
Ashton under Lyne manor, Lancashire, 49
Aston alias Church Aston manor, Shropshire, 42
Aylsham manor, Norfolk, 42

Badbury hundred court, Dorset, 39
Bamburgh manor, Northumberland, 23
Barry manor, Glamorgan, 27-8
Battle manor, East Sussex, 58
Beaminster Prima and Secunda manors, Dorset, 25
Bechill manor, Yorkshire, 74
Beeby manor, Leicestershire, 65
Birdbrook manor, Essex, 38
Birmingham, manor and borough, Warwickshire, 71
Bloxham Beauchamp manor, Oxfordshire, 25-6
Bloxham Fiennes manor, Oxfordshire, 25-6
Bodrugan manor, Cornwall, 45
Borough English, *see* ultimogeniture,
borough reeve, 72
boroughs, 9, 12, 39, 41, 49, 70–72
Boston borough and manors, lincolnshire, 9
Braintree, Essex, 70
Bramshall (*Bromshulf*) manor, Staffordshire, 35
Braunton manor, Devon, 13
bridewells, 40
bridge maintenance, 40
Bridport borough, Dorset, 71
Brighouse in Hipperholme, Wakefield, Yorkshire, 40
Brinkworth manor, Wiltshire, 8, 41, 52
Bromsgrove manor, Worcestershire, 80

Canford Magna manor, Dorset, 72
Casterton manor, Westmorland, 76
Cerne Abbas manor, Dorset, 77
Charlton manor, Wiltshire, 8
Chertsey Abbey, Surrey, 50
Child, John, 17
Chippenham manor and borough, Wiltshire, 56, 71-2
Chippenham manor, Cambridgeshire, 64, 80-1
Church Aston, *see* Little Ashton
church courts , 74
church gift, 32
Church Lawton manor, Cheshire, 8, 87
church officers, *see* parish officers
church rates, *see* parish rates
Coke, Edward, 43, 74
Collinson, Revd J., 13, 54-5
common fields, 9, 13, 16, 21, 23, 58-9, 77, 80

common land and grazing, *see also* waste, 9, 13-14, 19, 21, 23, 25, 28, 51-2, 54, 58, 69, 76, 79, 82
common law, 11, 74
common meadow, 13, 48
Compleat Court-Keeper, 43, 76
Congresbury and Puxton manor, Somerset, 13
conventionary tenure, 37
copyhold tenure, 20-1, 29, 31-2, 34, 37-8, 52-3, 58, 61, 64, 73, 76–78, 80-1
court baron, *see also* hallmoot, 13-14, 17, 19-21, 23, 24-8, 35-6, 38-42, 45, 48, 72, 76, 78, 89
court leet, 17, 19-21, 23, 28, 39-42, 48, 52, 59, 70-3, 78-80, 84-6, 90-1
Court of Augmentations, 15, 75
Court of Common Pleas, 74, 76
court of estrays, 19, 25
Court of Exchequer, 80
court of recognition, 19, 58
court of survey, 53, 58
Coventry manor and borough, Warwickshire, 70
Crediton manor, Devon, 56
Cumberland, 37
customs, 11, 20-1, 24-5, 31-2, 37, 43-4, 48–55, 57, 76-7, 81, 83

Danby manor, Yorkshire, 78-9, 86
deathbed transfers, 34
demesnes, 10-13, 15, 27, 37-8, 48, 51, 55-6, 58-9, 62, 68, 73, 78, 80-1
Denbigh manor, Denbighshire, 25
dissolution of monasteries, 7, 15, 84
Domesday, 9
Dorchester borough, Dorset, 71
Durham manors, County Durham, 70
Durweston, alias Durweston cum Knighton, manor, Dorset, 16, 60

Earls Colne manor, Essex, 38, 41, 49, 77, 82-3
enclosure, 13, 18, 23, 31, 38, 58, 62, 69, 74, 77-8, 81
enclosure maps, 69
enfranchisement, 34–6, 43, 69, 79, 91
Eton College, manors held by, 15, 84

fairs, 19, 41
Feckenham manor, Worcestershire, 68
Fonmon manor, Glamorgan, 27-8, 87
Fordington manor, Dorset, 33
freehold tenancies, 10-11, 13, 16, 21, 27-9, 31, 34, 37-9, 51, 59, 73-4, 76, 78, 81-2

Garsington manor, Oxfordshire, 11
gavelkind, 51, 74, 89

Giles Jacob, 43, 76
glebe land, 17
Glyndyfrdwy manor, Denbighshire, 4, 24
Gonville and Caius College, Cambridge, manors held by, 16
Gower Anglicana manor, Glamorgan, 12
Gower Wallicana manor, Glamorgan, 12
Great Corringham manor, Lincolnshire, 13
Great Stanmore manor, Middlesex, 43
Gretton manor, Northamptonshire, 27
Grishaugh manor, Norfolk, 42

Halifax, Yorkshire, 40
hallmoot, 19
Hanbury manor, Warwickshire, 10
Hardy, Thomas, 8
Harrington manor, Cumbria, 20
Hatton, Christopher, 62, 86
Havering manor, Essex, 25, 45, 49, 82
headborough, 19
headsilver (certum or cert money), 40
Hengrave, Suffolk, 15-16
heriots, 10, 21, 29, 32, 38, 49, 52-3, 54, 58, 61-2, 64, 78, 89
highway and bridge maintenance, 40-1, 73
Highways Act, 1555, 40
Hindringham manor, Norfolk, 74
Hipperholme, in Wakefield manor, 10, 40
Historic Manuscripts Commission, 78
Holdenby manor, Northamptonshire, 14
homage, 18, 20-1, 23, 25, 36, 45, 49, 52, 54, 69, 82, 90
Horton manor, Dorset, 23, 51
hundred courts, 39, 90
hundred penny (certum, cert money, head silver), 40
Hundred Rolls, 1279, 10-11, 87
Hunstanton manor, Norfolk, 16

Ibberton (Eberton) manor, Dorset, 60
Ilmington manor, Warwickshire, 64
inclosure, *see* enclosure *and* Inclosure Act
Inclosure Act, 1845, *see also* enclosure, 69, 77
inheritance customs, *see also* gavelkind and ultimogeniture, 16, 19, 21, 25, 27, 31-2, 34-5, 49-52, 54, 74, 80-1, 89

juries and jurors, 17-21, 25-6, 29, 31, 35-6, 41, 45, 49, 52, 72, 74, 82
Justices of the Peace, 40, 82

Kibworth Harcourt manor, Leicestershire, 17
Kilmersdon manor, Somerset, 34
Kingston Lacy manor, Dorset, 39
Kirkburton in Wakefield manor, 40
Kitson, Thomas, 15-16
knights' fees, 28-9

Land Registration Act, 2002, 80, 84, 92
Langton Wallis manor, Dorset, 62
Laxton manor and open field system,

Nottinghamshire, 13, 80, 85
leasehold, 11, 21, 27-8, 31, 34, 37-8, 51, 73, 76, 78, 87
Lestrange family, 16
Leven (*Leaven*) manor, Yorkshire, 19, 45
Lewin, John, 17
Lewin, Sarah, 17
Little Aston alias Church Aston, 42
Llancadle manor, Glamorgan, 27
Llanfyllin manor, Powys, 59
Loughborough manor and borough, Leicestershire, 70
Lytchett Minster, alias Lytchett cum Beere, manor, Dorset, 16, 87

Madeley manor, Shropshire, 56
Manchester manor, Lancashire, 8, 41, 70, 72
manor houses, 13-14
manorial documents, 7-9, 17-21
   accounts, 27, 42-3, 55-7, 70, 74-5
   court books, 24, 42, 52, 55
   court rolls, 7-8, 17, 20-1, 28, 31-3, 42, 52, 55, 69, 77, 80-1, 83-4
   custumals, 7, 10-11, 49-50, 52, 55, 83
   maps, 12, 64-5, 69, 80-1
   perambulations, 7, 9, 19, 43, 55, 68-9, 83-4
   presentments, 17, 19-23, 29, 35, 40-1, 43, 52, 54-5, 69, 71, 74, 82
   rentals, 7, 19, 25, 27-8, 37, 43, 55, 58, 62-4, 71, 80-4
   surveys, 7-8, 11, 19, 25, 27-8, 37, 43, 53, 55, 58-64, 69, 78, 80-4
   terriers, 81
Manorial Documents Register, 5, 7, 12, 37, 78, 83-4, 88, 92
manorial lords, 9-11, 13-17, 19, 20, 23-8, 31, 34, 37, 39, 42-3, 49-55, 58-9, 61-2, 64, 69-72, 74, 76-78, 80, 84
manorial officers and appointments (*see also* steward), 42-9
   ale taster (ale conner, alefiner), 19, 40, 45, 48-9, 70
   assesor of fines (*alias* affeeror), 20, 48-9, 53-4, 89
   bailiff, 8, 48-9, 54, 56, 69, 89
   barleyman, 49
   beadle, 12, 48, 89
   bellman, 49
   chimney inspector, 40
   constable, 19, 40-1, 45, 48-9, 72, 78
   grave (greive), 48
   hayward, 19, 48, 51
   hedgelooker, 49
   houselooker, 49
   inspector of weights, 49
   leather inspector or scrutineer, 21, 40, 48
   marsh reeve, 49, 82
   meat inspector, carniter or cargrave, 40, 45, 48
   messor (harvest officer), 48
   overseer of dolemoors, 13

pinder, 45, 48, 70
pound keeper, 48
recorder, 59
reeve, 19, 45-6, 48-9, 51, 56, 69, 72, 82, 90
scavenger, 19
shepherd, 48, 54
street master or commissioner, 70-1
sub-constable, 49
tithingman, 39-41, 46-8, 51, 61, 72
watchman, 48, 73
woodward, 48-9
Manorial Society of Great Britain, 78
manorial titles, registration, 78
markets, 14, 19, 41-2, 49, 56, 58, 70-2, 76, 78
marriage fines (merchets), 10, 90
marriages of tenants, 31, 34
meadow, 13, 23, 26, 37, 48, 58-9, 62, 69
Mere manor, Wiltshire, 25, 45, 52, 77
Mico, John, 17
Mico, Sarah, 17
mineral rights, 9, 14, 56, 76, 78, 80, 90
Monkton up Wimborne manor, Dorset, 29
Municipal Corporations Act, 1835, 41, 71

Nantconwy manor, Caernarvonshire, 74
New Alresford borough, Hampshire, 71
Norton Bavant manor, Wiltshire, 52
Nutborne manor, Suffolk, 79
Nywelond manor in Sherborne, Dorset, 28

Ogmore manor, Glamorgan, 74-5
Okeford Fitzpaine (*Ockford Fitzpaine*) manor, Dorset, 24, 53-4, 57, 59, 87
Orwell manor, Cambridgeshire, 80-1

parish officers, 40-1, 49
    churchwarden, 40, 51, 70, 73-4, 82
    overseer of the poor, 40, 82
    parish surveyor, 40
    vestryman, 82
parish rate, 77
parish registers, 80-2
parish vestries, 41, 73, 78, 82
Penmark manor, Glamorgan, 27-8, 87
Pennance manor, in St Budock, Cornwall, 66-7
Piddlehinton manor, Dorset, 15, 51
Poor law acts (Elizabethan), 40
poor rate and relief, 31, 40, 51, 73-4
Portland manor, Dorset, 32
Puddletown manor, Dorset, 53

quarries, 56, 58, 62
Quarter Sessions, 24, 40-1, 74, 77-8, 82, 90
quit rents, 10, 52, 56, 58, 71, 90

Raleigh, Carew, 45
Raleigh, Walter, 45
rectory or parsonage manors, 17
relief, 28
Repton, Humphry, 42
Rewe manor, Devon, 55, 63

St Catherine's manor in Ruislip, Middlesex, 17
services, commuted, 10, 11, 28, 51, 58, 62
Shaftesbury Abbey, 11
Shaftesbury borough, Dorset, 71
Sherborne, 84
shooting rights, 18
Shrivenham Stalpitts manor, Berkshire, 31
sporting rights, 78, 80
Stanton manor, Hertfordshire, 9
steward, 7, 8, 17-19-21, 25-7, 29, 32, 34, 42-5, 48-50, 52, 54-59, 64, 69, 74-8, 90
Stoneleigh manor, Warwickshire, 11
Sturminster Newton Castle manor, Dorset, 23
sub-tenants, 17, 48, 77
surrenders of customary land, 29-32, 37, 53-4

Taunton manor, Somerset, 54
tenancies, *see also* copyhold, conventionary tenancy, freehold, knights' fees, leasehold and tenant right, 10-11, 25, 27-30, 37-8, 49
tenant right, 37
Terling manor, Essex, 27, 41, 74, 81,-2
The Woodlanders (novel), 34
Three Castles manor, Gwent, 18-19
Turnpike Act, 1727, 41

ultimogeniture (Borough English), 50-1, 54, 89

view of frankpledge, 39
villeins and other unfree tenants, 10, 11, 37, 51

Wakefield manor, Yorkshire, 8, 10, 27, 39, 40, 48
Walsham Churchowse (Walsham Church House) manor, Suffolk, 61
Walsham-le-Willows manor, Suffolk, 61
Wareham manor and borough, Dorset, 8, 71, 91
waste, 13, 31, 37-8, 69, 71, 74, 77, 83
Whittlesey manor, Cambridgeshire, 74
widows, manorial rights of, 16, 25, 32-4, 48-53, 55, 80
Willingham manor, Cambridgeshire, 80-1
Winchester, bishop of, 71
woman as reeve, 45
women in manorial records, see also widows, marriage fines and marriage of tenants, 40, 45, 48
Woodlanders, The (novel), 34
Woodlands manor, Wiltshire, 25
wrecks, manorial rights to, 9, 14, 20, 56, 76-7, 90
Wrexham, land divisions within, 12
Wyke Regis manor, Dorset, 46-7

Zeals Aylesbury manor, Wiltshire, 25
Zeals Clevedon manor, Wiltshire, 25, 52

Lightning Source UK Ltd.
Milton Keynes UK
UKHW051115060223
416527UK00003B/31